CORRIGENDA AND ADDENDA TO TAKELMA TEXTS.

p. 11, at end—add: "* denotes theoretical forms"
p. 13, l. 10 (interlinear)—change "mourning" to "bereft of child"
p. 14, l. 11 (text)—change *abailiwilí*$^{u\varepsilon}$ to *abailiwilá*$^{u\varepsilon}$
p. 22, l. 8 (interlinear)—change "Di$^{\varepsilon}$lo^{u}mi^{1}" to "Di$^{\varepsilon}$lo^{u}mi^{i}"
p. 22, l. 10 (text)—change *xa*$^{\varepsilon}$*iyasgip!īlhi*$^{\varepsilon}$ to *xa*$^{\varepsilon}$*iyasgipīlhi*
p. 22, l. 10 (interlinear)—omit ", it is said"
p. 23, l. 3 (interlinear)—insert quotes (") before "Strings"
p. 24, l. 7 (text)—change *hã'xda*$^{\varepsilon}$ to *hãxda*$^{\varepsilon}$
p. 24, l. 11 (text)—change *mi*$^{i\varepsilon}$*s* to *mí*$^{i\varepsilon}$*s*
p. 25, l. 3 (text)—change *da-it!amák‘* to *de*$^{\varepsilon}$*idamá*$^{\varepsilon}$*k‘*
p. 25, l. 8 (text)—change *abaigini*$^{\varepsilon}$*k‘* to *abaiginí*$^{\varepsilon}$*k‘*
p. 26, l. 13 (text)—change *giní*$^{\varepsilon}$*k* to *giní*$^{\varepsilon}$*k‘*
p. 30, l. 11 (interlinear)—omit "to it"
p. 31, l. 14 (text)—change *mu*^{u}*xdánhi* to *mu*$^{u\varepsilon}$*xdánhi*
p. 32, l. 1 (interlinear)—change "holdidg" to "holding"
p. 41, footnote—change 3 to 31
p. 46, l. 1 (text)—change *t!i*^{i}*lā'p‘agit‘gwa* to *t!i*^{i}*lā'p‘igit‘gwa*
p. 50, l. 1 (text)—change footnote reference ^{2} to ^{5} (referring to p. 49)
p. 50, l. 2 (text)—change *he*$^{\varepsilon}$*īlemé*^{e}*k‘wana*$^{\varepsilon}$ to *he*$^{\varepsilon}$*īlemé*$^{e\varepsilon}$*k‘wana*$^{\varepsilon}$
p. 57, l. 4 (text)—change *desgwogwènt‘* to *desgwôgwènt‘*
p. 60, ll. 6, 7 (text)—change *nagaīk‘wa*$^{\varepsilon}$ to *nagaīk‘wa*
p. 61, l. 11 (text)—change *yalá*$^{\varepsilon}$*k* to *yalá*$^{\varepsilon}$*k‘*
p. 71, l. 4 (text)—change *hawa*^{a}*pi*^{i}- to *hawa*^{a}*p!i*^{i}-
p. 71, l. 15 (text)—change *īkwé*^{e}*xi* to *īk‘wé*^{e}*xi*
p. 71, l. 16 (text)—change *bayewé*^{i} to *bayewé*$^{i\varepsilon}$
p. 75, l. 3 (text)—change *xambilí*^{u} to *xambilí*$^{u\varepsilon}$
p. 76, l. 8 (interlinear)—change "with it" to "thereby"

p. 78, l. 4 (text)—change *heᵉdedáᵋ* to *heᵉdadáᵋ*
p. 78, note 2, l. 1—change "verb" to "aorist"
p. 87, l. 6—after "Coyote" insert: "Sharp-mouthed, sharp-clawed, s-cum matre copulans!" was said to him. "S-what do you say?"
p. 88, l. 9—change *wíⁱis* to *wíⁱs*
p. 92, l. 4—change *k!eméī* to *k!emèī*
p. 94, l. 2—change *nãk'wõk'* to *nãk'wôk'*
p. 95, l. 24—change "s-whats" to "s-what's"
p. 100, l. 1—change *yéũk'iᵋ* to *yèũk'iᵋ*
p. 101, l. 14—change ² to ¹
p. 105, l. 14—change ¹ to ²
p. 108, l. 8—change *disgot'õlha* to *disgot!õlha*
p. 109, l. 11—change *baᵃp'* to *baᵃp'*
p. 110, l. 3—change *p'elẽkwa* to *p'elẽk'wa*
p. 111, l. 7—change "the warriors assembled" to "he assembled the warriors"
p. 119, footnote—change "Atbabascan" to "Athabascan"
p. 120, l. 16—change *t'gaᵃ* to *t'gaᵃ*
p. 120, l. 17—change *gwī'ᵋne* to *gwī'ᵋne*
p. 122, l. 21—change *debü'ᵘᵋk'i* to *debü'ᵘk'i*
p. 124, l. 7—change *gingàt* to *gingàt'*
p. 127, note 6—add: *-t'git' ᵋiⁱt'eᵋ* is very likely transformed from *-t'gwat' ᵋeīt'eᵋ* "I am provided with. . .". See *T. L.*, p. 261, footnote
p. 134, l. 8—change *ópxakan* to *ópxak!an*
p. 142, l. 7—change *k'aiᵋlā'p'ak!i* to *k'aiᵋlā'p'ik!i*
p. 144, l. 17—change *sgaláuk,* to *sgaláuk'*
p. 146, l. 3—change *ág* to *gá*
p. 155, l. 14—change "did grow" to "he caused to grow"
p. 156, l. 21—change *káiᵋwa* to *k'áiᵋwa*
p. 171, note 9—change "grandfather" to "grandmother"
p. 173, l. 22—change *s·omlóholxaᵋs* to *s·omlohólxaᵋs*
p. 178, l. 18—change *ganàt'* to *ga nàt'*
p. 179, l. 28—change "Not in that fashion!" to "Do not say that!"

p. 182, l. 15—change *ts!a-imàt,* to *ts!a-imàt'*
p. 184, l. 15—change *gweliũs·i* to *gwel$^{\varepsilon}$iũs·i*
p. 188, l. 9—change *wi$^{\varepsilon}$wákdi'* to *wi$^{\varepsilon}$wák'di*
p. 189, note 4—change *Yūk'yák'wa* to *Yūk'yák'wa*
p. 191, note 8—change "did" to "will"
p. 194, l. 10—change *t'omomá$^{\varepsilon}$n* to *t!omomá$^{\varepsilon}$n*
p. 195, ll. 3, 10—change "shall" to "shalt"
p. 196, l. 18—change *sallatsàk'* to *sallats!àk'*
p. 206, l. 23—change *gwenai-á$^{\varepsilon}$s* to *gwena-iá$^{\varepsilon}$s*
p. 209, l. 4 from bottom—change "back" to "bark"
p. 222, l. 6—change *da^{a}* to *da^{a}-*
p. 229, ll. 4, 5—transpose "*iter.*" and "*usit.*"
p. 230, l. 21—change *ha$^{\varepsilon}$wi-* to *hawi-*
p. 230, l. 6 from bottom—change *ts·ai-m-* to *ts·!ai-m-*
p. 231, l. 6—change *ha-dak'* to *ha-dak'-*
p. 234, l. 9 from bottom—change "mensrtaul" to "menstrual"
p. 238, s. v. *yewei-* — add:

ba^{a}-		revive, be cured
ba^{a}-$^{\varepsilon}$i-yewe^{e}-n-(i-)		
: -ye^{e}w-an-	2 III	cure, bring to life

p. 239, l. 4 from bottom—add after "(from standing position)": "; be born"
p. 243, l. 13—change *-án-x-* to *-an-x-*
p. 253, l. 10—insert entry: *sēl* kingfisher
p. 263, note 1—change *yowo* to *yowo-*

UNIVERSITY OF PENNSYLVANIA
THE UNIVERSITY MUSEUM
ANTHROPOLOGICAL PUBLICATIONS
VOL. II No. 2

NOTES ON CHASTA COSTA PHONOLOGY AND MORPHOLOGY

BY

EDWARD SAPIR

PHILADELPHIA
PUBLISHED BY THE UNIVERSITY MUSEUM
1914

CONTENTS.

NOTES ON CHASTA COSTA PHONOLOGY AND MORPHOLOGY.

INTRODUCTION.

In a large part of southwestern Oregon and contiguous territory in northwestern California were spoken a number of apparently quite distinct Athabascan dialects. The territory covered by tribes or groups of villages speaking these dialects embraced not only a considerable strip of Pacific coast[1] but also much of the interior to the east (Upper Umpqua and Upper Coquille rivers, lower Rogue river, Chetco creek and Smith river); some of the tribes (such as Tolowa and Chetco) were strictly coast people, others (such as Galice Creek and Umpqua or Ą̧kwa[2]) were confined to the interior. While some of the Athabascan dialects spoken south of the Klamath in California, particularly Hupa and Kato, have been made well known to students of American linguistics, practically nothing of linguistic interest has as yet been published on any of the dialects of the Oregon-California branch of Pacific Athabascan. It is hoped that the following imperfect and fragmentary notes on one of these dialects may prove of at least some value in a preliminary way.[3]

[1] Outside of a few points in southern and southeastern Alaska (Cook Inlet, mouth of Copper river, Portland Canal) this is the only region in which Athabascan tribes have found their way to the Pacific.

[2] My ̧ denotes nasalization.

[3] The material for these notes was secured in a very incidental manner. While the writer was at work on Takelma in the latter part of the summer of 1906, he was living with Mr. Wolverton Orton, a full-blood Chasta Costa Indian. At odd moments Mr. Orton and the writer whiled away the time with Chasta Costa.

The Chasta Costa (or *Cis/ta q!wÁs/ta*) Indians, now gathered in Siletz Reservation in western Oregon, formerly occupied part of lower Rogue river; between them and the coast were other Athabascan tribes or villages of practically identical speech, above them to the east were the unrelated Takelma.[4] Among these tribes of nearly or quite identical speech were the *Yú̇*^{u}*/gwī* or Euchre Creek people, the *Tcê'/mê dA/ne* or "Joshuas" of the mouth of Rogue river, the *Dū/t'ú̇ dA/nī*, the *Mī/k!u/nú̇*^{u} *dA/nī*, and the *GwA/sá̇*. All these formed a linguistic unit as contrasted with the coast people (*ā/γṓs/ta* "lower tribes") or, as they are now commonly called by the Indians of Siletz, "Sol Chuck" Indians, a Chinook Jargon term meaning "salt water, coast" people; the dialect of these coast tribes was probably identical to all intents and purposes with Chetco. While Chasta Costa and Coast Athabascan are thus more or less distinct, they seem to have been mutually intelligible without very much difficulty, the coast dialect sounding merely somewhat "strange" and "drawn out" to a speaker of Chasta Costa. At least three other Athabascan dialects of this region, however, seem to have differed so much from Chasta Costa as to be but partly understood, if at all, by speakers of the latter; these are Upper Umpqua, Upper Coquille, and Galice Creek.

---

[4] It has already been pointed out (American Anthropologist, N. S., 9, p. 253, note 2) that there is reason to believe that J. O. Dorsey was incorrect in assigning the Chasta Costa villages above those of the Takelma (see his map in Journal of American Folk-Lore, III, p. 228). On p. 234 Dorsey gives a list of Chasta Costa villages.

PHONOLOGY.

VOWELS.

The vowels of Chasta Costa are *a*, *ā*, *e* (open as in English *met*), *ê* (long and open), *o* (close as in German *Sohn*), *ō*, *u* (apparently variant of *o*), *ū*, *i* (generally open), *ī*, and ᴀ (like *u* of English *but*); *ô* (short and open as in German *voll*) sometimes occurs after velars as variant of *o* (*sxô/lȧ* "five," cf. Hupa[5] *tcwō/la*), *ä* (as in English *hat*) occurs after velars as variant of *e* (*tsxȧ/xe* "child," cf. Carrier[6] *œzkhéhkhe* "children").

Vocalic quantity is of considerable importance in Chasta Costa, not so much etymologically as phonetically. On the whole, long and short vowels interchange on regular mechanical principles; open syllables (that is, syllables ending in a vowel) with long vowel regularly shorten this vowel when the suffixing of one or more consonants to the vowel makes the syllable closed. Examples of *a* thus varying with *ā* are:

dō/yác/t!a "I won't fly;" *dō/yát/t!a* "we won't fly" (cf. *dō/yȧ/t!a* "he won't fly")
dáθ/dā "he is sitting down" (cf. *dā/θ*ᴀ́*θ/dā* "I am sitting down")
*tc!ás*ʟ*/se* "he cries;" *tc!ác*ʟ*/se/t'e* "I shall cry" (cf. *tc!ā/θíl/se* "you cry")
*tc!a/γás*ʟ*/se* "they cry" (cf. *tc!a/γȧ/θil/se* "we cry")
nac/t!ô "I swim" (cf. *nȧ/tc!ī/t!ō* "you bathe")

---

[5] Hupa examples are taken from P. E. Goddard, "The Morphology of the Hupa Language," Univ. of Cal. Publ. Amer. Arch. and Ethn., 3.

[6] Carrier examples are taken from Rev. A. G. Morice, "The Déné Languages," Transactions of the Canadian Institute, I, pp. 170-212.

An example of ê shortened to *e* is:

nés/ts!Aɫ/ī "I am seen" (cf. *nê'/ts!Aɫ/ī* "he is seen")

Original long vowels may lose their quantity even in an open syllable, provided they are immediately followed or preceded by a syllable with relatively strong accent. Such are *tc!a-*, *na-*, and *ne-* in:

tc!a/γȧ/θil/se "we cry;" *tc!a/γásL/se* "they cry"
ne/nȯ/ts!Aɫ/ī "we are seen"
ɫá na/dit/t!ō "don't bathe;" (*na/dit/t!ō* is phonetically enclitic to strongly accented *ɫá*; contrast *nā/dít/t!ō/t'e* "you will bathe")

In general, however, stress accent cannot be said to be particularly well marked in Chasta Costa.[7] Each syllable is a fairly well-defined phonetic unit tending to hold its own against others, so that an approximately level accentual flow with but few peaks results. Such writings as *nā/dít/t!ō* and *tc!ā/θíl/se,* with apparent accent preceded by long vowels, are doubtless but imperfect renderings of forms with level stress on first and second syllables (they might perhaps better be written *nȧ/dìt/t!ō* and *tc!ȧ/θìl/se* with secondary accent on second syllable). It does not seem that every vowel in an open syllable is organically long; thus *e* in future *-t'e* and in *-de* of *t'wī/de* "everything" is regularly short. Many such cases are, however, probably only apparent, the short vowel being followed by a glottal stop; thus plural *ya-* of *ya/dAɫ/nī* "they make a sound" should doubtless be *ya'-*.

Short *a* of closed syllables is regularly reduced from long *ā*; original short *a* becomes *A* in a closed syllable. Examples of *A* thus dulled from original *a* are:

t'Ac/yÁc/t'e "I shall go" (cf. *t'e/θíc/ya* "I go;" *-yAc* = Hupa *-yauw̱*)

[7] Weak stress accent seems characteristic of Athabascan generally. Father Morice goes so far as to say, "there is no accent in Déné" (*op. cit.*, p. 173).

nā/xÁn/dō "eight, two less" (*nā/xA-* = Kato[8] *nąk/kaᵋ* "two")

dō/na/γÁct/xwī "I do not vomit" (cf. *na/γȧ/θAθt/xwī*[9] "I vomit")

t'Ál/dAc "he runs" (*-dAc* = Hupa *-dauw̲*)

γAn/na/'Ác "he will bring" (*-'Ac* = Hupa *-auw̲*)

t'é/An/γit/lAł "we are sinking" (cf. *t'e/nít/lat'* "we drown;" Hupa *-lat, -la* "to float")

Not to be etymologically confused with this *A* is inorganic *A*. Whenever a consonant is not followed by a definitely determined vowel and yet, for some reason or other, is not phonetically appended to the preceding syllable, it must begin its own syllable and takes an inorganic, in other words etymologically meaningless, *A*-vowel after it. This syllable may either be completed by a consonant of etymological value (such as first person singular *c*, verb class signs *ł, t, l*) never followed by a definite vowel or, if it is immediately followed by a syllable beginning with a consonant, this consonant is borrowed to complete the inorganic syllable (*-t* closes inorganic syllables preceding *d-, t!-, dj-, tc!-, ts!-, tθ!-, tc'-, L!-*), so that a doubled consonant results of which the first half is of no etymologic significance. In some cases, however, as before *γ-*, and in rapid speech generally, this inorganic consonant is not always distinctly heard; yet in syllabifying words Mr. Orton completed such inorganic syllables with a consonant with mechanical regularity. These syllables with inorganic vowel and consonant are characteristic not only of Chasta Costa but also of Hupa and Kato and doubtless other Athabascan dialects as well. The general phonetic tendency to speak in definite syllables and the further tendency to limit short vowels to closed syllables explain these characteristic Athabascan

---

[8] Kato examples are taken from P. E. Goddard, "Kato Texts," Univ. Cal. Publ. Amer. Arch. and Ethn., 5, 65–238; and "Elements of the Kato Language," ibid., 11, 1–176.

[9] *-ā-* may be secondarily lengthened from *-a-*.

developments. The quality of the inorganic vowel varies for different Athabascan dialects; it is *A* (*û*) in Kato as well as in Chasta Costa, *i* (*u* before voiced or voiceless *w*, *û* or *e* before post-palatal *k*-sounds) in Hupa, apparently *e* in Galice Creek, *æ* (probably identical with our *A*) in Carrier. Chasta Costa *xAt/t‘Ál/laɫ* "they sleep" is etymologically equivalent to *x/t‘/laɫ; x-*, third person plural prefix, cannot stand alone and is therefore followed by *A* and *t* borrowed from *-t‘-*, while *-t‘-* (verb prefix *t‘-* reduced from *t‘e-*, therefore not capable of combining with *x-* into *xAt‘-*) in turn needs a syllabifying *A* followed by *l* borrowed from *-laɫ*. Other examples of inorganic *A*, with and without following inorganic consonant, are:

> *t‘Ac/yÁc/t‘e* "I shall go" (*t‘A-* = *t‘-* reduced from *t‘e-*)
> *dō/yȧ/xAt/t!a* "they won't fly" (*xAt-* = *x-*)
> *nā/xÁt/dAl/nic* "they work" (*xAt/dA-* = *x/d-*, *d-* reduced from *de-*)
> *dȧ/xAn/nAt/t‘Ac* "they go to bed" (*xAn/nAt-* = *x/n-*)
> *t‘é/An/γAl/lAɫ* "he is sinking" (*γAl-* = *γ-*)

Many syllables with final consonant and *A*- vowel must be considered as radical or at least unanalyzable elements. In not all such cases is *A* a reduced form of *a;* where *A* seems a primary vowel, as shown by comparison with other Athabascan dialects, it seems best to consider it an organic element in the syllable, though it remains plausible that at last analysis it is but a reduced form of some fuller vowel. Thus, while *-yAc* has been shown to represent an original *-yac* (Hupa *-yauw̱*), *-t‘Ac* contains a primary *A*, as shown by comparison with Hupa *-tūw̱* "to lie down" (ultimately *-t‘Ac* is doubtless *-t‘*, reduced from *-t‘e*, and suffix *-c*).

Inorganic *A* sometimes becomes palatalized to *i*, though there is not enough material available to make it certain just when this change takes place. Examples of this secondary *i* have been found before *c* (but not before its developments *s* and *θ*) and *s* derived from *tc* (but not before original *s* or its development) when itself preceded by *m*, *n*, or *θ* (preceding *γ*, however, tends to preserve *A*). Examples are:

> *mís/ki*[10] "gull" (cf. Kato *bûtc/k'ai*ᵋ)
> *níc/ya* "I come" (*nic-* = cessative *n-* and first person singular *c*)
> *níc/dac* "I dance"
> *t'e/níc/lat* "I drown"
> *t'e/θíc/ya* "I go" (*θic-* = durative *θ-* and proncminal *c*; cf. *t'éθ/ya* "he goes" without vowel after *θ*)
> *tc!Aγ/γe/θíc/ya* "I eat"
> *γe/θíc/ī* "I saw him" (cf. *c/γéθ/ī* "he saw me")
> *θícł/sī* "I let him"

With *-θic-* contrast *-θAθ-* (both from original **-sAc-*) in *dā/θÁθ/dā* "I am sitting;" with *-θicł-* contrast *-sAsł-* (from original *-*sAcł-* and *-*sAcl-* respectively) in *tc!ā/sÁsł/se* "I am crying." *-γic-* was heard in *yā/γíc/t!a* "I fly," but as this is an isolated example (contrast *-γAc-* in *ná/da/γAct/t!ō* "I bathe" and *-γAcł-* in *γAcł/Áz* "I sneezed"), it seems possible that this form was misheard for *yā/γÁc/t!a*. Besides *-nic-* also *-nAc-* is met with: *dȧ/nAc/t'Ac* "I go to bed" and *nā/nÁc/An* "I stop him;" it is probable that in these forms *-nA-* is a reduced form of *ne-* (cf. Hupa *tcin/ne/tūw̱* "she goes to bed") and thus not directly comparable with *-ni-* of *-nic-*. Unaccented *A*, itself reduced from *a*, has in one case (*-yAc* "to go") been found further palatalized to *i*: *dō/t'Ác/yic* "I'll not go," *łá/t'ī/yic* "don't go!" (cf. *t'Ac/yÁc/t'e* "I shall go"); this *-yic* contracts with directly preceding *t'A-* into *-t'Ac*: *dō/t'Ác* "he won't go.[11]

Original Athabascan *ai* has in Chasta Costa become monophthongized to *ī*. Examples are:

> *ł/gī* "white" (cf. Kato *L/gai*)

---

[10] Should probably be *mísk!i'*.

[11] With this *-t'Ac* Kato *ta/cac* in *dō/ta/cō*ᵋ *ta/cac* "not anywhere I went" (P. E. Goddard, "Kato Texts," Univ. Cal. Publ. Amer. Arch. and Ethn., 5, No. 3, p. 182, l. 17) is in striking agreement.

mis/k!i'[12] "gull" (cf. Kato *bûtc/k'ai*ᵋ)
*hī*ⁱ[13] demonstrative "that" (cf. Hupa *hai*)

au as organic diphthong seems to occur but rarely in Athabascan. If *dō* "no!" (cf. Hupa *dau*) may be regarded as distinct from adverbial *dō* "not" (cf. Hupa *dō*), we would have an example of the parallel development of *au* to *ō* in Chasta Costa. Certain contractions that take place between *i* of first person plural *-it-* and second person plural *-ō-* with preceding vowels will be spoken of in discussing the pronominal prefixes.

One of the most striking phonological characteristics of Chasta Costa is the disappearance of an original *ŋ*[14] or of its representative, nasalization of preceding vowel. Its former presence can always be proved by comparison with other Athabascan dialects that, like Hupa, still preserve it. In the case of all vowels but inorganic *ᴀ* nasalization has left no trace whatever, original *ą̄* (from *āŋ*), *ę̂* (from *êŋ*), and *į̄* (from *īŋ*) being reduced to *ā*, *ê*, and *ī*; originally short vowels, on losing their nasalization and thus coming to stand in an open syllable, become lengthened, while originally long vowels in a closed syllable not only lose their nasalization but are shortened. Thus, a syllable *sī* may represent an original *sį̄* (or *sīŋ*) or *sį* (or *siŋ*), while *sil* may go back as well to *sį̄l* as to *sįl*. Examples of the absolute disappearance of an original *ŋ* are:

nā́/xe "you paddle" (*nā-* = **ną-*, cf. Hupa *nûñ/ya̩* "you are about")
dō/yā́/t!a "you won't fly" (*yā-* = **yą-*, cf. Hupa *yûm/mas* assimilated from **yûñ/mas* "you are rolling over")
tc!ál/se/t'e "you will cry" (*tc!al-* = **tc!ą-l-*; cf. *tc!áct/se/t'e* "I shall cry" with *-c-* "I" morphologically parallel to *-ᵋ-* "you")

---

[12] *ī* is here shortened to *i* because of following glottal stop.

[13] *ī*ⁱ denotes long *ī* with weakly rearticulated parasitic *i*. Such "pseudo-diphthongs" sporadically occur in Chasta Costa in lieu of ordinary long vowels.

[14] i. e., *ng* of English *sing*.

łá/na/γat/xwī "don't vomit!" (*γat-* = **γą̣t-*, cf. *γā-* from **γą̣-* in *na/γȧ/θit/xwī* "you are vomiting")
nét/ī "you are looking at him" (*net-* = **nẹt-* ; *-ī* = *-'ị*, cf. Kato *-īñ'* "to see")
łī "dog" (original Athabascan **łị*, **łiŋ*; cf. Hupa *ʟiñ*, Montagnais *l'iṇ*, Hare *tl'iṇ*, Loucheux *l'éṇ*, Carrier *łi*, old form *łœⁿn*[15])

Nasalized inorganic *ᴀ* seems to have acquired a palatal coloring *i*; this *i* then regularly developed to *ī* in open, *i* in closed syllables. It thus often seems as though Chasta Costa *ī*, *i* is the morphologic equivalent, for instance in second person singular forms, of Athabascan *η*, an equivalence, as has just been shown, due to secondary phonetic developments. Examples of *ī* < *ị* < *ᴀ* are:

t'e/θi/ya "you go" (*θī-* = **sᴀ-* ; cf. Hupa *na/siñ/ya* "you are going about")
ni/dac "you dance" (*nī-* = **nᴀ-*; cf. Hupa *niñ/yauw̱* "go!")
yú/wīs dī/nī "you whistle" (*dī-* = **dᴀ-*; cf. Hupa *da/din/ʟa* "run!" assimilated from **da/diñ/ʟa*
ná/tc!ī/t!ō "you swim" (*tc!ī-* = **kʸ!ᴀ-*;[16] cf. Hupa *na/kiñ/-yûñ* "come eat!")
yā/γi/t!a "you fly" (*γī-* = **γᴀ-*; cf. Hupa *ye/wiñ/ya* "you are going in")
yā/γi/t!a "it flies" (*γī-* = **γᴀ-*; cf. Hupa *na/win/ṯau* "it will settle down" assimilated from **na/wiñ/ṯau*)
t'i/lał "you are sleeping" (*t'ī-* = **t'ᴀ-*; cf. Hupa *tiñ/xauw̱/ne* "you take along")
verb stem *-sī* "to make" (cf. Hupa *-tcwiñ*)

---

[15] Morice, *op. cit.*, p. 210. Carrier has evidently undergone a development parallel to that of Chasta Costa. All northern Athabascan forms except Carrier (and Chipewyan) are taken from *R. P.* E. Petitot, "Dictionnaire de la langue Dènè-Dindjié."

[16] *kʸ!* is "fortis" palatal *k*, Hupa k_1, Morice's *q*.

Examples, in closed syllables, of *i*<*į*<*ᴀ̨* are:

tc!ā/θíl/se "you cry" (*θil-* = **sᴀ̨-l-*; cf. Hupa *na/dū/we/-sil/en/*[17]

nā/dít/t!ō/t'e "you will bathe" (*dit-* = **dᴀ̨-t-*; cf. third person *nā/dᴀ́t/t!ō/t'e*)

t'ā/γít/nā "you drink" (*γit* = **γᴀ̨-t-;* cf. third person *t'ā/γᴀ́t/nā*)

yā/γíl/gᴀθ "you climb" (*γil-* = **γᴀ̨-l-*; cf. third person *yā/γᴀ́l/gᴀθ*)

t'íl/xwᴀθ "you cough" (*t'il-* = **t'ᴀ̨-l-*; cf. third person *t'ᴀ́l/xwᴀθ*)

ne/ciɫ/ī "look at me!" (*ciɫ-* = **cᴀ̨-l-*)

Hupa *-ñ* (that is, our *η*) seems at times to correspond to Chasta Costa *-n*, but comparison with northern Athabascan dialects indicates that in such cases we are dealing with original *-n*. Thus, *nᴀn* "you," despite Hupa *niñ*, is shown to have original *-n* by Montagnais *nen* and Loucheux *nan*; *dᴀ́n/tc!i* "four," Hupa *diñk* (= *diηk^y!*), does not go back to original **dᴀ̨/k^y!i* but to **dᴀn/k^y!i* or **dᴀη/k^y!i* (*η* assimilated from *n*), as evidenced by Loucheux *tan*; *ɫa/cᴀ́n* "black" corresponds to Loucheux *del-zen*; similarly, *dᴀn* "in, at" must have original *-n* despite Hupa *diñ* and Kato *dûñ* (original **dᴀ̨* would have given Chasta Costa **dī*).

Consonants.

The consonantal system of Chasta Costa, like that of most Athabascan dialects, is characterized by a lack of labial stops, though *m* is common; *b* has been found in *bō/θí* "cat," a loanword from English *pussy*, but seems not to occur in native words (yet cf. *tcᴀ/pȧ/yu* "flower"). The consonants of Chasta Costa are: the labial nasal *m*; the dental stops *t'*, *d*, *t!*, and dental nasal *n*; the back stops *g*, *q'* (or *qx*), *q!*, voiceless spirant

[17] In Hupa *ñ* (or nasalization) disappears in closed syllables. In such forms Chasta Costa is etymologically more transparent than Hupa insofar as *-i-* is a reflex of original -ᴀ̨-, whereas Hupa *-i-* is the normal inorganic vowel.

x (as in German *Bach*), and voiced spirant *γ* (as in North German *Wagen*); the labialized back stops *k'w*, *g̣w*, *q!w*, and spirant *xw* (sometimes weakened to *hw*); the sibilants *s*, *c* (as in English *ship*), *θ* (as in English *thin*), and *z* (voiceless lenis, intermediate between *s* and English *z*, heard in *-ᴀz* "to sneeze"); the affricative palatal consonants *tc'*, *dj*, and *tc!*; the affricative alveolar consonants *ts*, *ts!*, and affricative dental consonant *tθ!*; the laterals *l*, *ł* (voiceless spirantal *l*, with *ʟ*, dorsal *t* followed by *ł*, as variant), and *ʟ!*; the glottal stop ('); the aspirate *h* (' at the close of a syllable); and the semivowels *y* and *w*.

Of these *t'*, *q'*, *k'w*, and *tc'* (English *ch*) are aspirated surds (*k'* is not found, *k'w* has been found but once and may be considered of doubtful occurrence); (*b*), *d*, *g*, *gw*, and *dj* are voiceless but lenis, intermediate acoustically between surds and sonants[18] (*dj* is intermediate between English *ch* and *j*); *t!*, *q!*, *tc!*, *ts!*, *tθ!*, and *ʟ!* are so-called "fortis" consonants, in other words, they are pronounced with simultaneous closure of glottis but are released before the release of the glottal chords. *q'*, *q!*, *g̣w*, and *q!w* (*g̣* has not been found, but very likely exists) are velar consonants; *k!* has not been found,[19] its place being taken by *q!*.[20] Of secondary origin are syllabically final *t* and *k*, which may be considered as voiceless stops differing from *t'* and *k'* in their lack of aspiration; they are etymologically equivalent to *d* and *g*. It is highly probable that also *w*, which does not frequently occur, is but a secondary development or acoustic variant of *γ* after *o*-vowels;[21] after *o*-vowels *γ* becomes labialized to γ^w, in which both *γ* and *w* elements are so weak that one is constantly in doubt as to whether he hears

---

[18] It is possible that these "intermediate" stops are sonant at their moment of release.

[19] Unless, as seems possible, *k* of *mís/ki* "gull" was misheard for *k!*.

[20] *q!* corresponds to Hupa k_3, *g* is Hupa k_2. *q!* is by no means as forcible a sound as is, e. g., Chinookan *q!*. There is something decidedly illusive about it; the velar stop element seems to be reduced to a minimum, the glottal catch element is very strongly marked, and a weak *x* seems at times to precede the velar stop (e. g., **q!ā/xᴀθ* "arrow"). Despite my familiarity with Chinookan *q!*, I did not often succeed in pronouncing Chasta Costa *q!* so as to satisfy Mr. Orton's ear. It may well be that *q!* is really "fortis" or glottalized *x* (*x!*); cf. Tlingit *s!*.

[21] In Hupa *γ* has become *w* in every case.

γ or *w* (thus *dō/γe-* becomes *dō/γʷe-*, *dō/ᵞwe-*; similarly, what was heard as *dō/wa-* may really be *dō/γʷa-*). However, *w* occurs also in *sā'/wᴀs/ts!é* "sandhill crane;" *wᴀs/xé* "good."

This consonant system is only in part a faithful representative of the original Athabascan system. Some consonants have become merged with others, while other consonants have kept distinct but have been changed in regard to place of articulation. Chasta Costa *m*, *t'*, *d*, *t!*, *n*, *g*, *q!* (*k!*), *q!w*, *γ*, *l*, *ł*, *ʟ!*, ', *h*, and *y* seem in practically every case to correspond to these same Athabascan sounds.

Athabascan *k'*, as also in Hupa, has become *x* in Chasta Costa:

> *xā'/tc'ú* "goose"[22] (cf. Hupa *xa*[23]; Applegate Creek *k'ą'/-tc'u*; Kato *k'a'*)
> *nȧ/xi* "two" (cf. Hupa *nax*; Montagnais *nak'é*[24])
> *ts!ȧ/xe* "woman" (cf. Carrier *tṣèkhè*[25])
> *tsxȧ/xe* "child" (cf. Carrier *œzkhéhkhe*)

Analogously to this change of *k'* to *x*, original Athabascan *k'w* has become *xw* (sometimes heard as *ḥw*) in Chasta Costa. This sound is preserved as such in Kato (*k'w*) and Chasta Costa (*xw*), but seems generally to have fallen together in other dialects with original *k'*. Examples are:

> *hwä* "foot" (cf. Kato *kweᵋ*; Carrier *ne-khé*; Loucheux *œkpè*)
> *na/γȧ/θᴀθt/xwį* "I vomit" (cf. Carrier *khu* "vomiting")

It seems, however, to persist as *k'w* in:

> *k'wᴀs/t'ȧ/ne* "six" (cf. Hupa *xōs/tan*)

Etymologically but not phonetically distinct, both in Hupa and Chasta Costa, from these secondary *x* and *xw* are

---

22 *-tcᵋu* is augmentative.
23 See Goddard, "Kato Texts," note 32.
24 Petitot's ' represents aspiration.
25 Father Morice represents "fortis" stops by means of points below characters.

original Athabascan *x* and *xw*. A good example of the latter is:

-*xw*ᴀθ "to cough" (cf. Carrier *xwœs* "cough," as noun)

Athabascan sibilants and sibilant affricatives (*ts* and *tc* sounds) have undergone various modifications in Chasta Costa. Original *s* has regularly become θ:

> θᴀ/γÁł "grizzly bear" (cf. Carrier *sœs-eʎœł* "brown bear")
> *t'e/θíc/ya* "I go" (cf. Hupa *te/sē/ya/te* "I am going away")
> *t'éθ/ya* "he goes" (cf. Hupa *tes/ya/te* "it is about to come")
> -*g*ᴀθ "to climb" (cf. Hupa -$k_2^a s$)
> -*xw*ᴀθ "to cough" (cf. Carrier *xwœs*)

Before *ł* (or its variant ʟ), however, *s* is regularly retained:

> *ts!ā/s*Á*s*ʟ*/se*[26] "I cry;" *tc!ás*ʟ*/se* "he cries;" *tc!a/γás*ʟ*/se* "they cry" (with these forms contrast *tc!ā/θíl/se* "you cry")
> *na/yés*ʟ*/sī* "he tells" (contrast *nā/θíł/sī* "you tell")
> *c*Á*sł/sī* "he lets me" (contrast *θícł/sī* "I let him")
> *c*ᴀ*sł/t'ȧł* "he kicks me" (contrast *θícł/t'āł* "I kicked him")
> *q!w*Á*t/das*ʟ*/nȧ* "it was lying on it"

Athabascan *ts* would, by analogy, have been expected to develop into *tθ* (as in Chipewyan), but θ seems to be regularly found instead:

> *θī* "head" (cf. Carrier *n-tsi* "your head;" Montagnais -*thi*;[27] Hare -*kfwi*; Loucheux -*tchi*[28]. Kato -*sī*ᵋ "head" seems to indicate that in Kato also, at least initially, *s* and *ts* fell together.
> θᴀ/γá "hair of head" (cf. Montagnais *éthi-ρa*[29])

---

[26] -*sas*ʟ- is assimilated from *-*sac*ʟ-, -*s*- being here prevented from becoming -θ- because of following -*s*- (before ʟ) of same syllable.

[27] i. e., -*tθi*. Petitot's *th* is *tθ*. In Hare *ts* (or its reflex *tθ*) developed into what Petitot writes *kfw*, perhaps to be understood as *kφ*, i. e., *k* plus bilabial *f*.

[28] Petitot's *tch* is our *tc*.

[29] Petitot's ρ is γ.

ł/θo "yellow, green" (cf. Montagnais *del-thop* "yellow;" Hare *dé-kfwoy* "yellow," Hupa *Lit-tso* "green;" Kato *L-tso* "blue")

In some cases *ts* seems to have become *s*:

sê "stone" (cf. Kato *se*; Hupa *tse*; Montagnais *thè*; Hare *kfwè*; Loucheux *tchi*; Carrier *tsé*)

As might be expected, Athabascan *ts!* has regularly become *tθ!* in Chasta Costa:

dā/de/θíl/tθ!i "we are sitting" (cf. Hupa *na/ya/del/tse,* i. e., *-ts!e,* "they lived as before")
tθ!Áθ/dā "story"

Athabascan *c* is normally preserved as such (e. g., *cī* "I"). However, it is assimilated to *s* before *s* and *ts!*:

s/ts!ī/dè "my sickness" (*c-* "my")
nés/ts!Ał/ī "I am seen (*-c-* "I")
As/sé/t'e "I shall cry" (from **Ac-*)
s/ts!An/na/'Ác "he will bring it to me" (*c-* "me")

Assimilation of **sAc* to *sAs* has taken place in:

tc!ā/sÁsL/se "I cry" (cf. *tc!ácL/se/t'e* "I shall cry")

Original **sAc*>**sic,* however, regularly developed to *θic*:

tc!Aγ/γe/θíc/ya "I eat"

Original **sAc,* after being assimilated to **sAs,* regularly shifted to *θAθ,* unless, as we have seen, it was protected by immediately following *ł*:

dā/θÁθ/dā "I am sitting" (from **dā/sÁc/dā*)
t'e/θÁθ/lał "I have been sleeping" (from **t'e/sÁc/lał*)
tc!eθ/t!ǒ "I swim across" (probably misheard for *tc!e/θAθ/t!ǒ*)

Original *s,* when immediately following *c,* also causes it to assimilate; *ss,* which thus results, is then regularly shifted to *θθ*:

yā/γÁθ/θeł "I threw" (from **yā/γÁc/seł*)

Athabascan *tc* (sometimes *tcw*?) is not retained in Chasta Costa, but appears regularly as *s*:

ł/sᴀk "red" (cf. Kato *ʟ/tcīk*; Loucheux *ditssig*)[30]
mís/k(!)i(') "gull" (cf. Kato *bûtc/k'ai*ᵋ)
sā'/wᴀs/ts!é "sandhill crane" (cf. Applegate Creek *tcā'/-wác/tc(!)e*)
-sī "to make" (cf. Hupa *-tcwiñ*; Kato *-tcī*; Chipewyan *-tsī*[31])
-se "to cry" (cf. Chetco *-swe*; Hupa *-tcwen*; Kato *-tce*ʻ; Carrier *-ssâ*)

Chasta Costa *sx* is found in:

sxô/lȧ "five" (cf. Hupa *tcwō/la*; Chipewyan *sa/sō/la/yai*ᵋ)

Athabascan *tc!* remains, *tc!* often being shifted, however, to *ts!* (or *s'*[32]):

tc!e- verb prefix "across the water" (cf. Hupa *tce-*, i. e., *tc!e-*, "down to the beach, out of the house;" Kato *tc'e-*; Chipewyan *ts'e-* "to a body of water")
-ts!ᴀn "toward, to" (cf. Hupa *-tciñ*, i. e., *-tc!iŋ*; Kato *-tc'ûñ*ᵋ; Chipewyan *-ts'ûn*)
ts!ł/de "sickness" (cf. Loucheux *tssik*, i. e., *ts!ik*)
*-s'at*ʻ "to be hurt" (cf. Hupa *-tcat*, i. e., *-tc!at*, "to be sick, to become ill")

There is still another set of sibilants in Chasta Costa, which go back to original palatalized (anterior palatal) *k*-sounds (g^y, k^y, $k^y!$). In Kato, Navaho, Apache, Chipewyan, and other Athabascan dialects, as in Chasta Costa, these have become affricative sibilants, without, however, falling together, as a rule, with the original Athabascan *tc*- consonants. In Chasta Costa, k^y has become *tc*ʻ, $k^y!$ has become *tc!* (this *tc!*

[30] Petitot's *tss* is our *ts!*.

[31] Chipewyan forms are taken from P. E. Goddard, "Analysis of Cold Lake Dialect, Chipewyan," Anthr. Papers Amer. Mus. Nat. Hist., vol. X, pt. II. Chipewyan forms taken from Petitot are referred to as Montagnais.

[32] It is quite likely that *tc!* and *ts!* are here merely auditory variants of *tś!* (*ś* is midway between *s* and *c*). In Kato *tc'*, *ts'* and *s'* also interchange.

does not vary, apparently, with *ts!*); for g^y I have no examples. Chasta Costa and Chipewyan are largely parallel in their development of Athabascan *ts*, *tc*, and k^y sounds:

Athabascan	Hupa	Chasta Costa	Chipewyan
dz			*dϑ*, *ϑ*
ts	*ts*	*θ*	*tθ*, *θ*
ts!	*ts!*	*tθ!*	*tθ!*, *θ'*
dj	*dj*		*dz*
tc	*tc*(*w*)	*s*	*ts*
tc!	*tc!*	*tś!*, *ts!*	*ts!*
g^y	g^y		*dj*
k^y	k^y	*tc*	*tc*
$k^y!$	$k^y!$	*tc!*	*tc!*

There are thus three distinct series of sibilant affricatives (and of sibilants) in Chasta Costa and Chipewyan, none of which is in direct accord with the original Athabascan sounds; Hupa, it is highly important to note, reflects the original sounds almost exactly.[33] Carrier, it would seem, has also preserved the k^y-series.

Examples of Chasta Costa *tc*ʻ from original k^y are:

áL/tcā/γî "big thing" (cf. Hupa *-kya/ō* "large;" Kato *-tca*^{y}, *-tca*ʻ "to be large")

---

[33] In his "Analysis of Cold Lake Dialect, Chipewyan," Goddard treats Chipewyan *ts* and *tc* as though they were one sound corresponding to Jicarilla and Navaho *tc* (p. 86). Examination of the various illustrative forms scattered throughout the paper, however, soon convinces one that Chipewyan *ts*, *dz*, and *ts!* correspond respectively to Hupa, Jicarilla, and Navaho *tc*(*w*), *dj*, and *tc!*; whereas Chipewyan *tc*, *dj*, and *tc!* correspond respectively to Southern Athabascan *ts*, *dz*, and *ts!* and to Hupa k^y, g^y, and $k^y!$. Thus, the Southern Athabascan *ts*- sounds represent both original *ts*- sounds and k^y- sounds; perhaps there is a phonetic difference that does not come out clearly in the orthography.
As for Kato, Goddard finds no difference between *tc*- sounds that go back to original *tc*- sounds and those that correspond to Hupa k^y- sounds ("Elements of the Kato Language," pp. 16, 51). However, deictic *tc*'-, corresponding to Hupa *tc!*-, varies with *ts*' and *s*', thus suggesting *tś!* as the true sound; on the other hand, *tc*'- (to indicate indefinite third personal object) corresponding to Hupa $k^y!$- occurs consistently as *tc*' (contrast examples of *tc*'-, *ts*'-, *s*'- on p. 50 with those of *tc*'- on p. 51). It seems plausible, then, that in Chipewyan, Chasta Costa, and Kato original k^y- sounds became true *tc*- sounds, while original *tc* sounds were shifted to *tś*- sounds (which are apt to be heard as either *ts*- or *tc*- sounds).

-tc'u augmentative suffix (e. g., *łi'/tc'ù* "horse," literally "big dog") (cf. Hupa *-kyō*; Kato *-tcō*)

Examples of *tc!* going back to Athabascan *kʸ!* are:

dʌn/tc!i "four" (cf. Hupa *diñk*, i. e., *diŋkʸ!*)
stc!ʌt/dé "seven" (cf. Hupa *xō/kit*, i. e., *-kʸ!it*)
tc!ásʟ/se "he cries" (cf. Hupa *kya/teʟ/tcwū* "it cried, i. e., *kʸ!a-*)
tc!- verb prefix indicating indefinite object (cf. Hupa *k-*, *ky-*, i. e., *kʸ!-*; Kato *tc'-*)

Athabascan possessed sonant sibilants (*z*, *j*) and sibilant affricatives (*dz*, *dj*). Of these sounds *z* has been found in Chasta Costa *-ʌz* "to sneeze;" *dj* is illustrated in several forms, but, as we shall see in a moment, does not in these go back to Athabascan *dj*. *dz* has not been found, though it may exist. *j*, as in Kato and Hupa, has become *c*:

ła/cʌn "black" (cf. Hupa *ʟū/hw̱in*<**-cin*; Kato *ʟ/cûnᵋ*; Jicarilla *ʟī/zī*; Nav. *ʟī/jin*; Chipewyan *del/zûn*; Loucheux *del-zen*)

Chasta Costa *dj* results from *t* (unaspirated) plus *y*:

q!wʌ́t/tc!ʌt/dja "table" (<**q!wʌt/tc!ʌt/ya* "whereon one eats;" *-ya* "to eat")
ya/da/γít/dja "we are ashamed" (<**ya/da/γít/ya*; cf. *yʌc* in *ya/dʌ́cł/yʌc* "I am ashamed")

Of the lateral consonants, only three (*l*, *ł*, and *ʟ!*) have been found in Chasta Costa. Original *dl* may have been preserved also, but Athabascan *dlō* was heard rather as *t* (unaspirated) plus *lō*:

γʌ́ct/lō "I laugh" (cf. Chipewyan *-dlō*, *-dlōk'* "to laugh") *-t-* is very probably third modal *-t-* here; while *-dlō* really appears as *-lō*. After *c* and *s*, *l* becomes *ł*:

nā/dʌ́cł/nic "I work" (cf. *nā/dʌ́l/nic* "he works")
ná/xwʌcł/ye "I play" (cf. *nā/xwʌ́l/ye* "he plays")
q!wʌ́t/dasʟ/nā "it was lying on it"

MORPHOLOGY.

Pronouns.

Independent personal pronouns:

cī "I"	*nê* "we" (probably contracted from **ne/he*; cf. Hupa *ne/he*)
nᴀn "you"	*nȯ/nè* "you" (plur.)
yū "he, that one" (really demonstrative)	*yů/nè*, *yún/nè* "they, those" (really demonstrative)

Examples of possessive pronouns are:

cíc/la "my hand" (*cic* is independent *cī* combined with possessive prefix *c-*; literally, "I my-hand")
nÁn/la "your hand" (that is, *nᴀn n-*, "you your-hand")
hi la "his hand" (*hī* is demonstrative)

c/na/γå "my eyes"

s/ts!ı/dè "my sickness, I am sick"
n/ts!ī/dé "you are sick"
nō/ts!ī/dé "our sickness, we are sick"
nō/ts!ī/dé/ha "your (pl.) sickness? are you (pl.) sick?" (*-ha* is interrogative)
xȯ/ts!ī/dè "their sickness, they are sick"

Many nouns, when limited by preceding possessive pronouns, suffix *-e*, as regularly in Athabascan. Thus, from *mᴀn* "house:"

cíc/mᴀnè "my house"
nÁn/mᴀne "your house"

A noun followed by another with suffixed *-e* is to be understood as genitively related to it. Examples are:

dᴀnê' lī/tc!e "person's dog" (*lī/tc!e* from *łī* "dog," with voicing of *ł-* to *l-*; cf. Hupa *Liñ* "dog," *xō/liñ/ke*, i. e., *xō/liŋ/kʸ!e* "his dog")

tAkÁc[34] *L!ōᵘ/le* "bowstring" (literally, "bow's string;" cf. Chipewyan *L'ūL* "rope," possessed form *L'u/le*)

gȧ/yu ts!ī/de "baby's sickness, baby is sick"

As reflexive possessive is used *xā/dAt-* (with *-ā/dAt-* cf. Hupa *a/d-*; Carrier *œdœd-*):

xȧ/dAt/lī/tc!é "his own dog" (used reflexively)

Of demonstrative pronouns there have been found:

hīⁱ "that, he" (cf. Hupa *hai*, indefinite demonstrative and article); *hȋⁱ/t!i* "that thing"

yū "that one" (cf. Hupa *yō* "that")

yṻ/ne, yún/ne "those, they"

m- "it" (cf. Hupa *m-*; Kato *b-*): *mAł* "with it"

de seems to be used as relative in:

dé ucL/tʻe "what I want"

This element is perhaps demonstrative in force and related to Hupa *de* in *ded* "this," *hai/de* "this."

Totality is expressed by *tʻwī* "all, everything" (cf. Hupa *a/tiñ* "all"). Compounded with this element are:

tʻwī/dé "everything" (*-de* is very likely related to Hupa *di-* in *dī/hw̲ō* "something," *dī/hw̲e/e* "nothing")

dȯ/tʻwī/dè "not everything"

tʻwi̇/dAn "everywhere" (literally, "all-at;" cf. Hupa *a/tin/-diñ* "every place")

Nouns.

Primitive non-descriptive nouns, as in all Athabascan dialects, are relatively frequent in Chasta Costa. Monosyllabic nouns are:

Body Parts.

la "hand" (cf. Hupa *-la*; Kato *-laᵋ*)

[34] Probably to be understood as *tʻAk/gÁc*.

hwä "foot" (cf. Kato *-kwe*ᵋ; Chipewyan *-ke*)
θī "head" (cf. Kato *-sī*ᵋ; Chipewyan *-θī, -tθī*)
-γa "hair" (in *θᴀγá* "head-hair;" cf. Kato *-ga*ᵋ "hair;" Chipewyan *-ɢa*, i. e., *-γa*)

ANIMALS.

tc!ac "bird"
łī "dog" (cf. Hupa *ʟiñ*; Chipewyan *ʟī*)

NATURAL OBJECTS.

sê "stone" (cf. Hupa *tse*; Kato *se*)
cā "sun" (cf. Hupa *hw̱a*; Kato *ca*)
łᴀt "smoke" (cf. Hupa *ʟit*; Kato *ʟût*)

CULTURE OBJECTS.

mᴀn "house" (cf. Hupa diminutive *min-tc* "hut")
ʟ!eł "matches" (originally doubtless "fire-drill;" cf. Chipewyan *ʟ'eʟ* "fire-drill")
gōθ "camass" (cf. Hupa *kos* "bulbs")
ʟ!ōᵘl-è "(its) string" (cf. Hupa *ʟōʟ* "strap;" Chipewyan *ʟ'ūʟ* "rope")

Primitive, at any rate not easily analyzed, nouns of more than one syllable are:

PERSONS.

dᴀn/né, dᴀnê' "person, man" (cf. Chipewyan *de/ne, dûn/ne*; Carrier *tœne*)
ts!á/xe "woman" (cf. Carrier *tṣèkhè*; Kato *tc'ek*)
dis/nê' "male" (with *-nê* cf. probably *-nê* of *dᴀnê'*)
sá/sᴀs "white man"
tsxá/xe "child" (cf. Carrier *œzkhéhkhe*; Kato *skī-k* "boys, children")
kéł/'è "boy" (perhaps misheard for *k!éł/'è*; cf. Kato *k'il/lek* "boy")
gá/yu "baby"

BODY PART.

na/γá "eye" (cf. Hupa *-na*; Kato *-na*ᵋ; Chipewyan *-na/ɢa*, *-na/ɢe*)

Animals.

θᴀγÁł "grizzly bear" (cf. Carrier *sœs-e^{d}œł* "brown or cross bear")

mís/k(!)i(') "gull" (cf. Kato *bûtc/k'ai$^{\epsilon}$*)

dís/ʟ!ac "fawn"

dᴀ/mel'/ké "pelican"[35]

nat/q^{x}í "duck" (cf. Kato *nắ^{a}/q'i*[36])

mī/tc'ắ/ts!ᴀl/nī "deer"

t'e/q!ô/lëc/l'e "mink"

sā'/wᴀs/ts!é "sandhill crane" (cf. Applegate Creek *tcā'/-wác/tc(!)e*)

tc!ał/tc!ús/dje "ruffled grouse, 'pheasant' "

θắ/gi "kingfisher"

dᴀs/nÁł "red-shafted flicker"

tθ!ᴀθ/nā/yał/tθ!óθ "hummingbird"

gī'c/tc!é "bluejay"

nā/ts!ǒ/łe "horned lark"

sǒ's/ga/ga "robin"

ts!ā/ts!úk "wren"

kᴀsís "barn swallow"

ga/łał/'é "crow"

Many of these animal names, as well as some of those that follow, are probably descriptive verb forms that have become stereotyped.

Plants.

tcᴀ/pắ/yu "flower"[37]

mī/t!al/tθᴀθ "arrow-wood"

ʟ!ō'/dé "tar-weed" (probably compounded with Athabascan *ʟ!ō'* "grass;" cf. Hupa *Lō/da-itc* "an herb")

tc!ᴀł/γat/ts!ė "sunflower(?)"

---

[35] This word is humorously used to refer to Democrats, Democrat and *dᴀ/mel'/ké* exhibiting some similarity in sound.

[36] This form was obtained independently.

[37] This word is remarkable as containing *p*, a sound that is normally absent in Athabascan.

dAl/si "pine" (cf. Kato *dûl/tcīk* "yellow pine," from *-tcīk* "red")

nȧ/L!e "pine-nut"

dA/nAc "manzanita" (cf. Hupa *din/nūw̱*; Kato *tûn/nûc* "manzanita berries;" Galice Creek *dé/rec*)

mAt/tc!í "cat-tail"

cAc/dȧ' "oak"

CULTURE OBJECTS.

xAnÁθ "canoe"

át/tca "pipe"

tc!A/θA/gAl "sandstone arrow-shaft scraper"

tA/kAc "bow" (probably *t'Ak/gAc*; cf. Kato *gąc* "yew")

ˣq!ȧ/xAθ "arrow"

det/t!é "arrow-point"

ABSTRACT.

tθ!Áθ/dȧ "story"

yů/wīs "whistling" (cf. Carrier *yuyuz* "whistling," as noun)

ts!ī/dé "sickness" (used with possessive pronouns to indicate "to be sick")

Several animals are designated by words ending in *-tc'u*, an augmentative suffix, "big" (cf. Hupa and Kato animal and plant names in *-kyō* and *-tcō* respectively). Such are:

łi'/tc'ŭ "horse" (literally, "big dog;" cf. Chipewyan *Līn/tcō*)

xā'/tc'ú "goose" (cf. Applegate Creek *k'ą́'/tc'u*. These words are formed from Athabascan *xa*: Chipewyan *xa* "goose;" Kato *ka'*)

dAc/tc'ú, *des/tc'ú* "grouse" (cf. Kato *dûc/tcō*, *dûs/tcō* "grouse")

t'ét/mō/tc'u "pigeon"

cu/dê'/tc'u "bald eagle"

θAθ/dA/łi/tc'u "owl"

łi/tc!ê/tc'u "red-headed woodpecker"

ga/sȧ'/tc'u "raven"

Nouns ending in *-t!ī* or *-t!īni* denote "one who has so and so." *-ni* is, likely enough, related to *-ne* of *dAn/né* "person;" *-ne* or *-n* is found in many Athabascan dialects as suffix denoting "person." Examples of *-t!ī(ni)* are:

łi/t!ī/nì "dog-owner"
dȯ/at/t!ī/ni, dȯ/at/t!ī "bachelor" (literally, "not-wife-having-person." *dō-* "not;" *at-*, i. e., *at!* "wife," cf. Hupa *ût̲* "wife," Kato *at'* "sister")

Examples of noun compounds consisting of two noun stems are:

θA/γá "head-hair" (shortened from *θī* "head" and *-γa* "hair." Cf. Chipewyan *θī/Ga*)
ga/łał g̣wȧ/yu "red-winged blackbird" (literally, "crow('s) brother-in-law." With this cf. Chipewyan *da/tsa/-tcel/le* "a small crow," literally, "crow younger-brother"[38]).

An example of a compound noun consisting of verb and noun is:

Al/Áz dAn/ne "sneezer" (literally, "he-sneezes person")

An example of a compound noun consisting of noun and adjective is:

tc!ac ł/θó/ē "bluebird" (literally, "bird blue")

A characteristic type of noun in Athabascan is formed by verbs which, while remaining strictly verbal in form, are used to refer to objects, in other words, are logically nouns. As has been already noted, several nouns of more than one syllable listed above as unanalyzable are doubtless, strictly speaking, verb forms. Quite clearly verbal in form are:

nāθ/L!ȯ "paper" (cf. *nał/L!ȯ* "he writes")
q!wÁt/daθt/gAc "table-cloth" (literally, "it lies *or* is thrown

---

[38] Goddard, *op. cit.*, p. 110.

down on top;" cf. Hupa *-k₂as*, i. e., *-gas*, "to throw," and *wes/kas* "it lay"[39])

q!wÁt/tc!At/djà "table" (literally, "thereon it is eaten")

mAł/t'é/tc!At/ts!Al/lec "smoking materials" (literally, "therewith it is smoked")

Numerals.

1. *ła, łȧ^a/ca* (cf. Hupa *La*; Kato *La/ha^ε*)
2. *nȧ/xi* (cf. Hupa *nax*; Kato *nąk/ka^ε*); *nȧ/xi la* "two hands"
3. *t'ȧ/γi* (cf. Hupa *tak*, i.e. *t'ak!*; Kato *tak'*; Chipewyan *ta, ta/Ge*
4. *dÁn/tc!i* (cf. Hupa *diñk*, i. e. *diŋk^y!*; Chipewyan *dī/Gī*)
5. *sxô/lȧ* (cf. Hupa *tcwō/la*; Chipewyan *sa/sō/la/Gai^ε*)
6. *k'wAs/t'ȧ/ne* (cf. Hupa *xōs/tan*)
7. *stc!At/dé* (cf. Hupa *xō/kit*, i. e. *-k^y!it*)
8. *nā/xÁn/dō* (="it lacks two, two less")
9. *łán/dō* (="it lacks one, one less")
10. *hwê'/θe*

Of numeral adverbs there were recorded:

łát/dAn "once" (cf. Hupa *na/diñ* "twice," *min/Lûn/diñ* "ten times")

ła/mé/q!e/ca "in one time"

Adjectives.

Of adjectives, or verb stems with adjectival significance, there have been found:

wAs/xé, wAs/xȧ "good;" *wAs/xé łī* "dog is good"

txAs/xé/la "rich" (*-la* is verbal suffix)

dů/An/dê "bad" (evidently verbal in form. *dū-, dō-* is negative; *-dê* probably misheard for *-t!ê* "to be, exist;" cf. Hupa *ûn/te*, i. e. *An/t!e* "there is")

---

[39] Goddard, *op. cit.*, p. 281.

ÁL/tcā/γī "big thing" (cf. Hupa *-kya/ō* "large;" Kato *-tcaG*)
ł/gī "white" (cf. Hupa *-L/kai*; Kato *-L/gai*)
ła/cÁn "black" (cf. Kato *-L/cûnʿ*; Chipewyan *del/zûn*)
ł/sAk "red" (cf. Kato *-L/tcīk*)
ł/θo "yellow, green" (cf. Hupa *Lit/tsō* "green;" Kato *-L/tsō* "blue")

"White," "black," "red," and "yellow, green" are characterized by prefixed *ł(a)*-, which is common as adjectival prefix also in other Athabascan dialects.

Adverbs.

Adverbs of place are:

xun "there" (cf. Hupa third personal pronoun *xōñ?*):
xún tʿe/θì/ya "there you go"
hīⁱ xún tʿeθ/ya "there he goes"
txún/la "where?":
txún/la tʿe/θì/ya "where are you going?"
dō/dAt "nowhere" (cf. Hupa *-dit-* in *hai/dai/dit/diñ* "where;" *dō-* is negative)
dAk/gé "up" (cf. Hare *tègè*):
dAk/gé θicł/tʿāł "I kicked him up"
mā̍ᵃ/dAn "on edge" (*-dAn* is postposition "at;" *māᵃ-* < **mą-* < **maŋ-*; cf. Hupa *niL/man* "each side")

Adverbs of time are:

xat "then" (cf. Hupa *xat* "yet, right")
xā "quickly" (cf. Hupa *xa* "yet")
xun/dé "tomorrow" (cf. Hupa *yis/xûn/de* "tomorrow"):
xun/dé dō/wa/γÁc/ī "I'll see him tomorrow"
xún/dè tθ!Aθ/dā nAł nácł/sī "tomorrow story to-you I-shall-tell"
xun/dé tʿAc/yAc "tomorrow I'll go")

t'wi/dAn "always" (literally, "all-at"):

t'wi/dAn t'Al/dAc "he always runs"

t'wi/dAn As/se "I always cry"

xAL/ts!i/dAn "this evening" (doubtless misheard for *xAL!-*; *-dAn* is postposition "at." Cf. Hupa *xû/Le* "in the night"):

xAL/ts!i/dAn dō/wan/γAc/ī "I'll see you this evening"

Modal adverbs are:

dō negative (cf. Hupa *dō*):

dō/t'Ac "he won't go"

dō/t'Ac/yic "I'll not go"

dō/yȧ/t!a "he won't fly"

dȯ/As/se "I'm not crying"

dō/nȧ/dAcL/nic "I'm not working"

dō/γÁc/ī "I didn't see him"

dō/nécł/ī "I'm not looking at him"

dȯ/ucL/t'e "I do not want"

dō/na/γÁct/xwī "I do not vomit"

ła prohibitive:

łá "don't!"

łá/t'ī/yic "don't go!"

ła/γi/ī "don't see him!"

łá/nā/xwil/ye "don't play!"

łá/na/dit/t!ō "don't bathe!"

łá/na/γat/xwi "don't vomit!"

dō/dȧ/q!e "unable"

dȯ/LAn "not much" (cf. Hupa *Lan* "much," *dō/Lan* "little")

dō/wi/la "of course" (cf. Hupa *dōñ* "it is," *he/dōñ* "at least")

dō/lȧ emphatic negative (really verbal in form, "to cease;" cf. Hupa *-lan*, *-lûñ* with negative prefix *dō-* "to quit, leave, desist"):

dō/lȧ c/γī/ī "you didn't see me"

cȯᵘ/djī "all right" (cf. Hupa *nū/hw̲ōñ/ᵃx* "properly"?)
cAł/q!we "to be accustomed to":
cAł/q!wé na/dAct/t!ō "I'm used to bathing"
t!īⁱ/xun "to keep on:"
t!īⁱ/xún ne/cAł/ī "he keeps looking at me"
θAk/gwe "in fragments"
hō future prefix (more properly intentive):
hō/yā/γíc/t!a "I'll fly"
hō/tc!ÁsL/se "he wants to cry"
hȯ/il/ī γit/lō "stop laughing!"
dō/wa future prefix (probably with dubitative coloring):
dō/wa/c/γī/ł̄ⁱ/t'e "you'll see me"
s/ts!ī/dé dō/wa/Al/lê' "I'll get sick" (literally, "my-sickness will-become")
dō/wa/nȧ/yan/nAł "he will upset them"
dō/wa/łt'át/nAł "they will go to pieces"

Postpositions.

Athabascan is characterized, among other features, by the use of a considerable number of postpositional elements of chiefly local force. They are appended to nouns or pronominal, numeral, or adverbial stems; less often to verb forms, in which case they have subordinating force. Chasta Costa examples are:

-dAn "at" (cf. Hupa *-diñ*):
xAL(!)/ts!ī/dAn "this evening"
t'wī/dAn "everywhere" (literally, "all-at")
łát/dAn "once" (cf. *ła-* "one")
mȧᵃ/dAn "on edge"
ał/dAc/nī/dAn "when I tell him" (literally, "I-tell-him at")[40]

---

[40] Similarly in Hupa *-miL* "when," as verb suffix, is doubtless simply pronominal *-mi-* plus postposition *-L* "with."

-*ł* "with, to" (cf. Hupa -*L*; Kato -*L*):

xAnAθ/ł nác/xe "I paddle canoe" (literally, "canoe-with I-paddle")

tθ!Áθ/dă nAł nácł/sī "I tell you story" (literally, "story you-with I-make")

tθ!Áθ/dā cAł na/yésL/sī "he tells me story" (literally, "story me-with he-makes")

mAł/t'é/tc!At/ts!Al/lec "wherewith it-is-smoked, materials for smoking" (*mA-ł-* "therewith;" cf. Kato *bûL* "with it;" Hupa *miL* "with, in")

This same -*ł* is probably also found attached to verbal prefix *a-* (used in verbs of saying):

ał/dAc/nł/dAn "when I tell him" (cf. Hupa *aL/-tcit/den/ne* "he talked to")

-*ts!An* "toward" (cf. Hupa -*tciñ* "toward;" Kato -*tc'ûñ*ʿ "to, toward"):

s/ts!An/na/'Ác "to-me he-will-bring-it"

-*me* "in" (cf. Hupa -*me* "in;" Kato -*bī*ʿ "in"):

mAn/mé "in house"

-*me/q!e* "in, around in" (compounded of -*me* and -*q!e*; cf. Chipewyan -*k'e* "on"):

mAn/mé/q!e "around in house"

ła/mé/q!e/ca "all in one time" (cf. *ła*, *łă*ᵃ*/ca* "one")

Verbs.

As in other Athabascan dialects, the typical Chasta Costa verb consists of one or more adverbial prefixes, which may be followed in order by a deictic or third personal element, a first modal prefix, a second modal element, a first or second person subjective element, and a third modal element or "class" sign; these, not all of which need of course be present, are then followed by the verb stem itself. The stem often ends the verb form, but may be followed by one or more enclitic elements of modal or syntactic force. The verb form is frequently preceded by an adverb or postposition which, while best considered as a non-integral part of the verb, forms a rather close syntactic unit with it. A pronominal object, if present, comes after an adverbial prefix but before a first modal element. Thus, the verb form *t'ā/γȧ/θōt/nā/hā* "do you (plur.) drink?" consists of seven elements: *t'ā-*, an adverbial prefix referring to water; *γā-*, a second adverbial element; *θ-*, a second modal element of durative significance; *-ō-*, second person plural subjective pronominal element; *-t-*, a third modal element, probably intransitive in force; *-nā*, verb stem "to drink;" and *-hā*, an enclitic interrogative element. The various elements that go to make up verb forms will be taken up in the order indicated.

Adverbial Prefixes. *ā-*, *a-*, *'ᴀ-* used with verbs of saying, doing, and being (cf. Hupa and Kato *a-*):

> *ȧ/djᴀn* "he says"
> *aɫ/dᴀc/niɫ/dᴀn* "when I tell him" (for *-ɫ-*, see under Postpositions)
> *dȯ/dᴀt 'ᴀn/t!e* "there is not anywhere"

This *a-* is probably equivalent to an indefinite object, "something," indicating what is said or uttered without definitely referring to it. This comes out rather clearly on comparison with a form like *yů/wīs dᴀcɫ/nī* "I whistle" (literally, "whistling I-utter"), where no indefinite object *a-* is required, what is uttered being specifically referred to by *yů/wīs* "whistling." That *a-* is somewhat in a class by itself as compared with other adverbial prefixes is indicated by its being followed in forms with indirect object by postpositive *-ɫ-*.

yā-, *ya-* "up (in the air)" (cf. Hupa *ya-*; Kato *yaᵋ-*):

> *yā/γᴀ́cɫ/gᴀθ* "I climb"
> *yā/γᴀ́θ/θeɫ* "I threw"
> *yā/γíc/t!a* "I fly"

It is not clear what significance is to be attached to *ya-* in:

> *ya/dᴀ́cɫ/yᴀc* "I am ashamed"
> *ya/da/γít/dja* "we are ashamed"

ye- "into enclosed space (including mouth)" (cf. Hupa *ye-*; Kato *ye'-*, *yī'-*)

ye/γát/ne/la "he bit it"

dā-, *da-* "sitting or lying on something above ground" (cf. Hupa and Kato *da-*):

dā/θÁθ/dā "I am sitting down"

dā/de/θíl/tθ!i "we are sitting down"

då/nʌc/t'àc "I go to bed"

q!wÁt/daθt/gÀc "it lies thrown down on top," i. e. "table-cloth")

q!wÁt/dasʟ/nà "it was lying on it"

t'e- "in the water" (cf. Hupa *te-*; Kato *te'-*):

t'é/ʌn/γʌc/lʌł "I am sinking in the water"

t'e/níc/lat "I drown"

t'ā- referring to water (cf. Hupa and Kato *ta-*):

t'ā/γÁct/nā "I drink"

tc!e- "across a stream" (cf. Hupa *tce-* "out of;" Kato *tc'e-* "out of;" Chipewyan *ts'e-* "used of approach to a body of water"):

tc!e/θít/t!ō "I swim across"

ʌn- implies disappearance or undoing (cf. Chipewyan *ʿa-*, *an-* "away," implies "desertion or abandonment"):

t'é/ʌn/γʌc/lʌł "I am sinking in the water"

dō/wá/ʌn/nā/yan/nʌł "he will upset them"

an- "back, hither" (cf. Chipewyan *ʿā-* *ʿan-*, *ai-* "back, toward home"):

an/γi/ał "come here!"

tc!ā-, *tc!a-* of unknown significance (cf. Hupa *kya-*[41]):

tc!ā/sÁsʟ/se "I cry" (cf. Hupa *kya/teʟ/tcwe* "she heard it cry")

tc!ásʟ/se "he cries"

se'- used with verb of smiling:

sé'/γʌt/lō "he smiles" (cf. *γÁt/lò* "he laughs")

---

[41] Goddard lists forms in *kya-*, i. e., *kʸ!a-*, under *ky-;* see *op. cit.*, p. 90. It seems better however, to keep them apart.

tc!ō- of unknown significance (cf. Hupa *kyō-*[42]):
tc!ō/γít/siʟ/la "he pointed with his finger"
né/tc!ūc/lec "I'll bet you"[43]

u- of unknown significance (cf. Hupa verbs in *ō-*[44])
dȯ/ucʟ/t'e "I do not want"
dé/ucʟ/t'e "what I want"

nā-, *na-* indefinite movement on surface of ground or water; horizontality (cf. Hupa and Kato *na-*):
nᴀn/náθ/yā/la "he went around it"
s/ts!ᴀn/na/'ᴀ́c "he'll bring (it) to me"
γᴀ́n/na/ᴀ́c/t'e "he will bring here"
nā/nɨ/ᴀn "stop him!"
nȧ/γa "is going about, living"
ɬ/t'ɨ γᴀn/na/'à "he brags" (literally, "high, important he-has")
nȧ/xwᴀcʟ/yè "I play"
nā/dᴀ́cʟ/nic "I work"
dō/wa/nȧ/yan/nᴀɬ "he will upset them"
nāc/ʟ!ȯ "I write"
xᴀnᴀθ/ɬ nác/xe "I paddle canoe"
nac/t!ȯ "I swim, bathe"
na/tc!ɨɬ/de "you wash"
nȧ/dᴀcɬ/dè "I washed myself"
nā/dᴀ́t/t!ō/t'e "he'll bathe"
nā/xᴀt/dᴀ́l/eɬ "they'll bathe"
tθ!ᴀ́θ/dà cᴀɬ nā/θɨl/sī "story to-me you-told, caused"

na- "back again" (cf. Hupa and Kato *na-*), followed by third modal *-t-*:
na/γȧ/θᴀθt/xwɨ "I vomit"

γᴀn- of uncertain significance (cf. Hupa *wûn-* "to pursue

[42] Goddard lists forms in *kyō*, i. e., *kʸ!ō-*, under *ky-;* see *op. cit.*, p. 90. Perhaps *kʸ!ō* is compounded of *kʸ!-* and *ō-*.

[43] This *tc!ū-* is probably better explained as deictic *tc!-* followed by future imperative *ū-;* see note 86.

[44] Goddard, *op. cit.*, p. 115.

or seek something; to attempt something by persistent effort"):

γÁn/na/Ác/t'e "he will bring here"

ł/t'i γAn/na/'à "he brags" (perhaps "important he-seeks-to-have")

ne- of unknown significance:

nécł/ī "I'm looking at him" (cf. *γe/θic/ī* "I saw him")

nés/ts!Ał/ī "I am seen"

xw(*A*)- of unknown significance:

nȧ/xwAcL/yè "I play"

xwÁcL/ī "I believe (it)"

xwAn/né/θiL/ya "you win" (see under first modal *ne-*)

γā- γa-, (*γ*) refers apparently to "mouth":

ye/γát/ne/la "he bit it" (*γat-* may, however, have been misheard for *γAt-*, with second modal *γ-*; see note 92)

na/γȧ/θAθt/xwī "I vomit"

łá/na/γat/xwī "don't vomit!"

t'ā/γȧ/θit/nā "we drink"

t'ā/γít/nā "you drink" (or is *γ-* here second modal prefix?

Verbal prefixes of local force which are doubtless primarily postpositions and which are prefixed to adverbial prefixes proper are:

nAn- "around" (cf. Hupa *-nat*; Kato *-na*):

nAn/náθ/yā/la "he went around it"

q!wAt- "on, on top" (cf. Hupa *-kût* "on;" Kato *-k'wût'* "on"):

q!wÁt/tc!At/dja "whereon one eats, table"

q!wÁt/daθt/gÀc "it lies thrown down on top, table-cloth"

q!wÁt/dasL/nȧ "it was lying on it"

DEICTIC PREFIXES. Under this head are grouped a small number of quasi-pronominal elements of third personal reference which regularly come after adverbial prefixes, if any of these are present. They cannot be grouped with first or second personal subjective elements, as their position is quite distinct from these; first and second modal prefixes may come between. Of deictic elements there have been found:

tc!- denotes lack or indefiniteness of object of transitive verb (cf. Hupa *k-*, *ky-*, i. e. *kʸ!-*; Kato *tc'-*[45]):

tc!ᴀγ/γe/θíc/ya "I eat" (i. e. without specific object being designated; cf. Hupa *yik/kyū/wiñ/yan* "it ate")

q!wᴀ́t/tc!ᴀt/dja "whereon one eats, table"

nắ/tc!ił/ʟ!ō "you write" (cf. Hupa *na/kis/Lōn*, i. e. *na/kʸ!is/ʟ!ōn* "she made baskets")

nắ/tc!ī/t!ō "you swim, bathe"

na/tc!ít/de "you wash" (cf. Kato *te'/na/tc'ûs/dēɢ* "he washed it")

tc!ᴀt/t'ít/θᴀł "we wash ourselves" (cf. Hupa *wa/kin/nin/seʟ* "it was heated through")

mᴀł/t'é/tc!ᴀt/ts!ᴀl/lec "wherewith it is smoked" (somewhat doubtful, as *tc!-* here follows first modal prefix *t'e-*; but see note 77)

tc!ᴀ́ł/t!ō "he sucks" (cf. Kato *tc'iʟ/t'ōt* "[make] it suck")

It is possible that in this last example *tc!-* is third personal subjective (cf. Hupa *tc-*, i. e. *tc!-*; Kato *tc'-*, *ts'-*, *s'-*), as suggested by *ᴀcł/t!ô* "I suck" with its lack of *tc!-* prefix. No other plausible case, however, of third personal subjective *tc!-* is available, so that its existence in Chasta Costa must be considered doubtful as yet.

Generally third person singular subjective forms are distinguished by the lack of any pronominal prefix, but in certain

---

[45] Goddard, *op. cit.*, p. 51.

cases deictic elements are found which are clearly third personal (subjective) in value. These are:

dj- (cf. Hupa *tc-*, i. e. *tc!-*; Kato *tc'-*, *ts'-*, *s'-*):

á/djAn "he says" (verb-stem *-n*; cf. Hupa *aL/-tcit/den/ne* "he talked to them")

djÁn/la "he says" (cf. Hupa *tcin* "they say;" Kato *tc'in*)

It is quite likely, however, that *djAn* is to be explained as from **dyAn* (*dy*, as we have seen, becomes *dj*), in which *d-* is first modal prefix (cf. *dí/nī* "you make a sound") and **yAn* is reduced from **yen* (*ye-* as below; *-n* to say).

ye-, *ya-* (cf. Hupa *y-*, *yī-* referring to other than adult Hupa; Kato *yī-*):

nAł na/yéL/sī "to-you he-tells" (contrast *nácł/sī* "I tell")

cAł na/yésL/sī "to-me he-tells" (with second modal prefix *s-*, *θ-*; contrast *nā/θíł/sī* "you tell")

ya/q!éθ/ya[46] "he eats" (contrast *tc!Aγ/γe/θíc/ya* "I eat")

x-:

tc!é/xAθ/t!ō "he swims across" (contrast *tc!e/-θít/t!ō* "you swim across")

This *x-* seems to have no parallel in Hupa or Kato (is it connected with third person objective *xō-* of Hupa, *k͟w-* of Kato?). Were it not that *-t!ō* "to swim, bathe" is used only of singular subjects, one might surmise that *x-* is really plural *xA-* (see below).

Among deictic elements are further to be reckoned certain prefixes that serve to indicate either plurality as such or more specifically third personal plurality. These are:

ya- (cf. Hupa *ya-*; Kato *yaᵋ-*):

yú/wīs ya/dil/nī "we whistle" (contrast *yú/-wīs dAcł/nī* "I whistle")

---

[46] *q!e-* was very likely misheard for *γe-*.

yů/wīs ya/dʌɫ/nī "they whistle" (contrast *yů/wīs dʌɫ/nī* "he whistles")

γā-, *γa-*:

tc!a/γȧ/θil/se "we cry" (contrast *tc!ā/sʌ́sʟ/se* "I cry")

tc!a/γásʟ/se "they are crying" (contrast *tc!ásʟ/se* "he cries")

tc!ā/γȧl/se/t'e "you (pl.) will cry" (contrast *tc!ȧl/-se/t'e* "you (sing.) will cry")

xʌ- third person plural (apparently not found in either Hupa or Kato; but cf., without doubt, Chipewyan *he-* "used for dual or plural of verbs in third person"):

yā/xʌγ/γi̇/t!a "they fly" (*yā/γi̇/t!a* "it flies")

dō/yȧ/xʌt/t!a "they won't fly" (*dō/yȧ/t!a* "he won't fly")

xʌs/sé/t'e/ha "will they cry?" (*ʌs/sé/t'e/ha* "will he cry?")

dō/xʌ́s/se "they're not crying" (*dȯ/ʌs/se* "he's not crying")

nā/xʌ́t/dʌl/nic "they work" (*nā/dʌ́l/nic* "he works")

c/xʌ/γéθ/ī "they saw me" (*c/γéθ/ī* "he saw me")

na/xʌt/da/γʌ́l/eɫ "they are bathing"

t'é/ʌn/xʌγ/γʌl/lʌɫ "they sink in the water" (*t'é/ʌn/γʌl/lʌɫ* "he sinks")

xʌt/t'ʌ́l/laɫ "they are sleeping" (*t'ʌ́l/laɫ* "he is sleeping")

dā/xʌ́n/nʌt/t'ʌ̀c "they went to bed" (*dȧ/nʌt/t'ʌ̀c* "he went to bed")

xʌt/t'ʌ́l/xwʌθ "they cough" (*t'ʌ́l/xwʌθ* "he coughs")

xʌ/ʌ́l/ʌz "they sneeze" (*ʌl/ʌ́z* "he sneezes")

First Modal Prefixes. Under this term are comprised a small number of rather frequently occurring elements which regularly come after both adverbial prefixes and deictic elements, but precede another set of modal elements (second modal prefixes) which are to be taken up shortly. Their meaning is rather colorless. Besides their position they have this peculiarity in common, that they lose their vowel in indefinite tense forms (such as have no second modal prefixes: *θ*-, *γ*-, or *n*-) and are thus reduced to single consonants. They are:

t'e- (definite tenses), *t'*- (indefinite tenses) seems to indicate durative activity (cf. Hupa *te*-; Kato *te*-, *t*-):

t'e/θíc/ya "I go;" indefinite: *dō/t'ʌ́c/yic* "I'll not go;" *t'ī/yʌ́c/t'e* "you must go"

t'ʌ́cʟ/dʌc "I run" (indefinite)

tc!ʌt/t'ö/θʌł "you (pl.) wash yourselves" (indefinite)

t'/γi̇/ī "he looks around" (indefinite; but see note 69)

t'e/θʌ́θ/lał/la "I've been sleeping;" indefinite: *t'ʌ́c/lał* "I'm sleeping"

t'ʌ́cł/xwʌθ "I cough" (indefinite)

mʌł/t'é/tc!ʌt/ts!ʌl/lec "wherewith it is smoked" (as following *tc!*- is deictic, it is more likely that *t'e*- here is adverbial prefix, not first modal; see note 77).

de- (definite tenses; *da*- before *γ*-), *d*- (indefinite tenses) meaning unknown (cf. Hupa *d*-, *dū*-; Kato *de*-, *d*-):

ał/dʌc/ni̇/dʌn "when I tell him" (indefinite)

yů/wīs dʌcł/nī "I whistle" (indefinite)

c/na/γä dīⁱ/s'at' "my-eyes hurt" (definite; cf. Hupa *dū/win/tcat* "it got sick")

ná/da/γʌct/t!ö "I bathe;" indefinite: *nā/dʌct/-t!ö'/t'è* "I'll bathe"

na/da/γíl/êł "we are bathing;" indefinite: *nā/-díl/eł* "we'll bathe"

nā/dʌ́cʟ/nic "I work" (indefinite)

nå/dʌcł/dè "I washed myself" (indefinite)

ya/dʌ́cł/yʌc "I am ashamed" (indefinite)

ya/da/γít/dja "we are ashamed" (definite)

dā/de/θíl/tθ!i "we are sitting down" (definite)

γe- (definite tenses), *γ-* (indefinite tenses) meaning unknown:

tc!Aγ/γe/θíc/ya "I eat"

ya/q!éθ/ya "he eats" (*q!e-* is probably misheard for *γe-*)

γe/θi̇/ī "you saw him;" indefinite: *dō/wa/γī/i̇/t'e* "you'll see him"

γéθt/lō "he breaks into laughter;" indefinite: *γÁt/lō* "he laughs"

an/γi̇/al "come on!"

This *γe-*, *γ-* should not be confused with second modal *γ-*, which will be taken up presently. Two first modal prefixes (*t'-* and *γ-*) occur in *t'/γi̇/ī* "he looks around;" that *γ-* is not second modal here is indicated by parallel definite forms with *γe-* (see *γe/θi̇/ī* above), further by weak form *t'-* of first prefix (definite tenses require *t'e*)[47]

ne- (definite tenses), *n-* (indefinite tenses) meaning unknown (cf. Hupa *ne-*, *n-*; Kato *ne-*, *n-*; Chipewyan *ne-*, *nū-*):

xwAn/né/θiL/ya "you win" (cf. Kato *kûn/ne/sīL/yan* "you win")

då/nAc/t'Àc "I go to bed" (indefinite; cf. Hupa definite: *tcin/nes/ten* "he lay")

n/da' "it is, stays" (indefinite; cf. Kato definite: *tc'n/nes/dai* "he sat down")

nā/nÁc/An "I stop him;" *nā/ni̇/An* "stop him!" (indefinite)

n/dō "it is not" (indefinite; cf. Kato *n/dōᵋ/ye* "there is none")

This *ne-*, *n-* is not to be confused with second modal *n-*, which occurs only in definite tenses.

SECOND MODAL PREFIXES. These comprise three consonantal elements (*θ-* or *s-*; *γ-*; and *n-*) which are used only in definite tenses and which have reference, as far as any definite

---

[47] Moreover, *t̔e-* in definite tenses seems regularly followed by second modal *θ-*, not *γ-*. Yet *-ī-* of *γī-* causes difficulty; see note 69.

significance is ascertainable at all, to what may be termed range or span of activity, but not to tense as such. *θ-* (*s-* in certain forms) is durative or continuative in force (cf. first modal *t'e-*, which is regularly followed by *θ-*); *n-* is cessative, marking the end of an activity or marking an activity which is conceived as the end point of a previous activity (e. g., "to come" as contrasted with durative "to go"); *γ-* is the most uncertain, being apparently inceptive or momentaneous in some cases, but clearly not so in others.[48] They are, it seems, mutually exclusive elements. In practice their use seems largely determined by the prefixes that precede. *n-* and *γ-* always begin their syllable, being completed either by *-ī-* (<**-iŋ-*) or by subjective pronominal or by third modal elements, which are joined to them by means of *-i-* or inorganic *-ᴀ-*; *θ-* (*s-*) is similarly joined to following subjective pronominal elements, if one is present, otherwise it forms part of the preceding syllable.

Examples illustrating *θ-* (*s-* before *ł*, *ʟ*) are:

- *t'e/θíc/ya* "I go;" *t'éθ/ya* "he goes" (cf. Hupa *te/sē/yai* "I went away")
- *nᴀn/náθ/yā/la* "he went around it"
- *tc!ᴀγ/γe/θíc/ya* "I eat;" *ya/q!éθ/ya* "he eats" (contrast Hupa *yik/kyū/wiñ/yan* "it ate" with *w-*)
- *tc!e/θít/t!ō* "you swim across" (contrast *na/da/-γít/t!ō* "you bathe")
- *dáθ/dā* "he is sitting down" (cf. Hupa *sit/dai* "he lived")
- *dā/de/θíl/tθ!i* "we are sitting down" (cf. Hupa *de/sōʟ/tse/te* "you will stay")
- *tc!ā/θíl/se* "you (sing.) cry" (contrast Hupa *win/-tcwū* "you have cried")

---

[48] Goddard somewhat doubtfully assigns inceptive force to its Hupa cognate *w-;* in Kato its cognate *g-* seems clearly inceptive only in certain verbs; while in Chipewyan Goddard ascribes continuative value to *g-*. It would be worth while making a somewhat extended comparative study of the second modal prefixes of Athabascan, which form one of the most difficult but at the same time important chapters of its grammar.

γe/θíc/ī "I saw him" (cf. Hupa *te/sūw̲/iñ* "I am going to look")
nā/θił/sī "you told story" (cf. Hupa *na/seʟ/tcwen* "I made")
t'e/θɨ/lał/la "you've been sleeping" (cf. Hupa *nit/te/sil/lal/le* "you would go to sleep")
θícł/t'āł "I kicked him" (contrast Hupa *ye/tcū/-wiʟ/taʟ* "they landed" with *w*-)
na/γȧ/θit/xwɨ "you vomit"
γe/θᴀ́θt/lō "I break into laughter"
ʟȧθ/ā/la one was (= *ʟā* "one" plus *θ/'ā/la*; cf. Chipewyan *ϑe/ʿā* "was there")
q!wᴀ́t/daθt/gᴀ̀c "it lies thrown down on top, table-cloth" (cf. Hupa *wes/kas* "it lay")
q!wᴀ́t/dasʟ/nȧ "it was lying on it"
xwᴀn/né/θiʟ/ya "you win" (cf. Kato *kûn/ne/-sīʟ/yan* "I win")

Examples illustrating *n*- are:

níc/ya "I come" (cf. Hupa *nei/yai* "I came")
níc/dac "I dance" (cf. Kato *nûc/dac* "I will dance")
t'e/nɨ/lat "you drown" (cf. Kato *tc'n/nûl/lat* "it floated there")

Examples illustrating *γ*- are:

γɨ/dac "he dances" (cf. Kato *tc'/gûn/dac/kwañ* "he had danced")
yā/γᴀ́cł/gᴀθ "I climb" (cf. Hupa *ya/wiʟ/kas* "he threw up")
yā/γɨ/t!a "it flies" (cf. Hupa *na/win/t̲au* "it will settle down")
ná/da/γᴀct/t!ȯ "I bathe"
na/da/γíl/êł "we are bathing" (cf. Chipewyan *na/ī/ginʟ/ūʟ* "take through the water")

t'é/ᴀn/γᴀc/lᴀł "I'm sinking in the water" (cf. Hupa *da/na/wil/laʟ* "it was floating there")
γᴀcʟ/ᴀ́z "I've been sneezing"
tc!ō/γít/siʟ/la "he pointed with his finger"
ya/da/γít/dja "we are ashamed"

Subjective Pronominal Prefixes. There are three persons and two numbers (singular and plural), making six persons in all. The third persons, as we have seen, are indicated either by the absence of a pronominal element or by deictic prefixes which come between the adverbial prefixes and the first modal elements. There thus remain four persons (first person singular and plural, second person singular and plural) for treatment here. In the definite tenses the pronominal elements are appended to the second modal elements, with which they form a syllable, an inorganic *ᴀ* or *i*, if necessary, serving to connect them. In the indefinite tenses the pronominal elements are appended to whatever element (adverbial prefix, deictic element, or first modal prefix in reduced form) happens to precede them. They never begin their syllable except in the comparatively small number of cases in which the verb form, indefinite in tense, has nothing preceding the pronominal element or, in the case of the third person, nothing preceding the third modal prefix or verb-stem. When this happens, the second person singular and plural and the first person plural stand at the very beginning of the verb; the first and third persons singular, however, begin with an inorganic vowel *ᴀ*-.

First Person Singular -c- (cf. Hupa -w̱-; Kato *-c-*; Chipewyan *-s-*):

t'e/θíc/ya "I go"
θícʟ/t'āł "I kicked him"
níc/ya "I come"
dȧ/nᴀc/t'ᴀc "I go to bed"
t'é/ᴀn/γᴀc/lᴀł "I am sinking in the water"
γᴀ́ct/lō "I laugh"

yā/γÁcł/gAθ "I climb"
t'ÁcL/dAc "I run"
nac/t!ȱ "I swim, bathe"
Acł/t!ȱ "I suck"
AcL/Áz "I sneeze"

In definite tenses with *θ-* or *n-* as prefix the inorganic vowel connecting these elements with *-c-* is regularly *i*; this is evidently due to the palatal quality of the *-c-*. In definite tenses with *γ-* as prefix, however, the normal inorganic vowel, *A*, is found, due, no doubt, to the velar position of the prefix. In the indefinite tenses the connecting vowel, if required, is always *A*. Where we have *nAc-* we are dealing with first modal *ne-*, reduced to *n-*, plus *-c-*, not with second modal *n-* plus *-c-*; contrast definite *níc/ya* with indefinite *dȧ/nAc/t'Àc*.

Before *s-* sibilants *-c-* is assimilated to *-s-*:

dȱ/As/se "I'm not crying" (<**Ac/se*)

θic- goes back to original **sic-* or **sAc-*. When *-c-* came to stand before a dental consonant (*d, t, l*), it was assimilated to *-s-*, and the inorganic vowel preceding it assumed the form *A*; this **sAs-* then regularly became *θAθ-*:

dā/θÁθ/dā "I am sitting"
γe/θÁθt/lō "I break into laughter"
na/γȧ/θAθt/xwį "I vomit"
t'e/θÁθ/lał/la "I've been sleeping"

Before third modal *-ł-*, *θic-* seems to be regularly retained (cf. *θícł/t'āł* above; *θícł/sī* "I make"). Secondary *sAs-*, not shifted to *θAθ-*, is found, however, before *ł(L)* when this element is secondarily changed from third modal *-l-*:

tc!ā/sÁsL/se "I cry"

That *sAsL-* here is equivalent to **sAsl-*<**sAcl-* is indicated by *tc!ā/θíl/se* "you cry;" contrast *θíł/t'āł* "you kicked him," *θícł/t'āł* "I kicked him."

It is to be carefully noted that *-c-* (or its reflexes *-s-*, *-θ-*) is in Chasta Costa found in both definite and indefinite tenses. There is no trace of an element corresponding to the Hupa *-e-* (*-ē-*), Kato *-ī-*, Chipewyan *-ī-*, which are found in forms of definite tenses. It is quite probable that the *-c-* of the indefinite forms was extended by analogy.

Second Person Singular i- (cf. Hupa *-ñ-*, i. e. *-η-*; Kato *-n-*; Chipewyan *n-*, *ne-*, or nasalization of vowel:

t'íl/dᴀc "you run"
t'ā/γít/nā "you drink"
nā̇/tc!ił/ʟ!ō "you write"
na/da/γít/t!ō "you bathe"
nā/dít/t!ō/t'e "you'll bathe"
yā/γíl/gᴀθ "you climb"
ya/díl/yac "you are ashamed"
nā/θī̇ł/sī "you made, told"
nā/xwíl/ye "you play"
xwíl/ī "you believe it"
xwᴀn/né/θiʟ/ya "you win"
t'íl/xwᴀθ "you cough"

In all these cases the *-i-* connects a following third modal element (*-ł-*, *-l-*, or *-t-*) with a preceding prefix. Examples of *-i-* beginning its own syllable are:

īl/Áz "you sneeze"
hō̇/il/ī "stop!"

If there is no third modal element, the *-i-*, lengthened to close *-ī-*, closes its syllable:

dā/nī̇/t'ᴀc "go to bed!"
t'ī̇/lał "you are sleeping"
dā/θī̇/dā "you are sitting"
yā/γī̇/t!a "you fly"
dō̇/ī/se "you do not cry"

This *i-*, *ī-*, is only secondarily the second person singular subjective element. The original element was doubtless *-η-* (cf. Hupa), which was reduced to nasalization of preceding vowels; the inorganic vowel, when nasalized, took on *i-* timbre. Finally, when nasalization disappeared, the *i-* timbre alone remained as the reflex of original *-η-*. Where, in many indefinite tense forms, the nasalized vowel was other than an inorganic one, there was nothing left of the *-η-*:

dō/yȧ/t!a "you won't fly"
nȧ/xe "you paddle"
néł/ī "look at him!" (cf. *nécł/ī* "I'm looking at him")

In such cases the second person singular fell together with the third, as in *dō/yȧ/t!a* "he won't fly."

First Person Plural (*i*)*t-*[49] (cf. Hupa *it/d-*, *-d-*; Kato *d-*; Chipewyan *-t-*, *-d-*[50]):

t'ít/lał "we are sleeping"
tc!ᴀt/t'ít/θᴀł "we wash ourselves"
t'e/nít/lat "we drown"
dā/nít/t'ᴀc "we went to bed"
γe/θít/ī "we saw him"
yā/γít/t!a "we fly"
t'é/ᴀn/γit/lᴀł "we are sinking in the water"
dȯ/it/se "we are not crying"

In Hupa and Kato regularly, and in Chipewyan often, the first person plural subjective pronominal prefix begins its syllable; in Chasta Costa it regularly ends its syllable, unless it has to stand at the beginning of the verb form, when it constitutes a syllable by itself (cf. *dȯ/it/se* above; *dō* "not" is independent adverb rather than prefix).

---

[49] *t* is here unaspirated, and is thus etymologically identical with *d*.

[50] In Father Legoff's Montagnais paradigms *-id-* or *-it-* often, in fact regularly, appears; *-i-* seems, as in Chasta Costa, to be organic.

If the prefix preceding the pronominal element ends in a vowel, the *-i-* disappears:

dō/yát/t!a "we won't fly"

This does not mean, however, that this *-i-* is to be considered an inorganic vowel, as is the case in Hupa *it/d-*. If *-it-* is followed by third modal *-t-*, both *-t-* elements combine into a single *-t-*, and all that is left of the pronominal prefix is the *-i-*:

t'ā/γȧ/θit/nā "we drink" (contrast *t'ā/γáθt/nā* "they drink")

If the third modal element is *-ł-* or *-l-*, *-t-* disappears and *-ł-* is changed to *-l-*; thus the first person plural of *ł-* verbs and *l-* verbs is always formed alike. In Hupa and Kato third modal *-ł-* regularly becomes *-l-*, but *d-* is preserved; hence Hupa *dil-*, Kato *dûl-*. In Chipewyan, however, as in Chasta Costa, *-ł-* not only becomes *-l-*, but *-t-* disappears. For Chasta Costa this means that the second person singular and first person plural of *l-* verbs is identical, provided, of course, that there is no deictic prefix of plurality in the latter and that the verb stem does not change for the plural. Examples of *l*-verbs are:

dā/de/θíl/tθ!i "we are sitting" (cf. Chipewyan *de/θīl/θ'ī* "we are sitting")
nā/dīl/nic "we work" (cf. *nā/díl/nic* "you work")
t'íl/xwAθ "we cough" (cf. *t'íl/xwAθ* "you cough")
nā/xwīl/ye "let us play" (cf. *nā/xwíl/ye* "you play")
īl/Áz "we sneeze" (cf. *īl/Áz* "you sneeze")
na/da/γíl/êł "we are bathing;" *nā/díl/eł* "we'll bathe"
tc!a/γȧ/θil/se "we cry" (cf. *tc!a/θíl/se* "you cry")

Examples of *ł-* verbs are:

yū́/wīs ya/dil/nī "we whistle" (cf. third person plural: *ya/dÁł/nī*)
nȧ/tc!il/L!ō "we write" (cf. *nȧ/tc!ił/L!ō* "you write")

If, in an indefinite tense form, the pronominal element is preceded by a prefix ending in a vowel and is, besides, followed by third modal *-ł-* or *-l-*, both *-i-* and *-t-* have to disappear and there is nothing left of the pronominal element except, in the case of *ł-* verbs, the change of *-ł-* to *-l-:*

> *nél/ī* "let us look at him!" (cf. *néł/ī* "look at him!")
> *tc!ā/γél/se*, very likely misheard for *tc!ā/γál/se* "we'll cry" (cf. definite: *tc!a/γȧ/θil/se* "we cry")

Second Person Plural ō- (cf. Hupa *ō'-*; Kato *ō'-*; Chipewyan *ō'-*):

> *t'ȯ/lał* "ye sleep"
> *t'e/θȯ/lał* "ye have been sleeping"
> *t'e/nȯ/lat* "ye drown"
> *yā/γȯ/t!a* "ye fly"
> *t'é/ᴀn/γō/lᴀł* "ye sink in the water"
> *t'ā/γȧ/θōt/nā* "ye drink"
> *dȯ/ō/se* "ye are not crying"

No aspiration was heard after *ō* in Chasta Costa. This does not seem due to faulty perception, as *l-* verbs keep their *-l-* after *ō-*, whereas, under similar circumstances, Hupa, Kato, and Chipewyan change *-l-* to *-ł-* (*ō'-l-* becomes *ōł-*). Indeed, in Chasta Costa *ł-* verbs change their *-ł-* to *-l-* after second person plural *ō-*. Examples of *ō-* before *l-* verbs are:

> *nā/dȯl/nic* "ye work"
> *na/da/γȯl/êł* "ye bathe;" *nā/dȯl/eł* "ye will bathe"
> *t'ȯl/xwᴀθ* "ye cough"
> *nā/xōl/yé/le* "ye play" (for *-xwōl-*)
> *ōl/ᴀ́z* "ye sneeze"

Examples of *-ł-* becoming *-l-* after *ō-* are:

> *ya/dȯl/nī* "ye utter, make a sound" (cf. third person plural *ya/dᴀ́ł/nī*)
> *ne/xȯ/ōl/ī* "ye look at him" (cf. *néł/ī* "you're looking at him")

When, in an indefinite tense form, *ō*- is preceded by a prefix ending in *a*, *a* and *ō* contract to long *ā* (which, it would seem, remains long even in closed syllables):

> *dō/yȧ̆/t!a* "ye won't fly" (<**yaō*ʻ-; cf. third person singular *dō/yȧ̆/t!a* with original *yā*-; and second person singular *dō/yȧ̆/t!a*<**yą*-<**yaη*)
>
> *tc!ā/γȧ̆l/se/t*ʻ*e* "ye will cry" (cf. definite: *tc!a/γȧ̆/θōl/se* "ye cry;" and contrast *tc!ā/γál/se* "we'll cry" with short -*a*-)

Third Person. As already noted, the third person, apart from possible deictic prefixes, is marked by the absence of any pronominal element. If the element preceding the third modal prefix or the stem consists of a consonant which must begin its syllable, an inorganic -ᴀ- is found between the two; if a third modal prefix is absent, the syllable preceding the stem is closed by a consonant borrowed from the first consonant of the stem. Examples of third persons with -ᴀ- before a third modal prefix are:

> *ya/d*ᴀ́*l/y*ᴀ*c* "he is ashamed"
> *t*ʻᴀ́*l/d*ᴀ*c* "he runs"
> *nā/xw*ᴀ́*l/ye* "he plays"
> *yā/γ*ᴀ́*l/g*ᴀ*θ* "he climbs"
> *yů̇/wīs d*ᴀ*ł/nī* "he whistles"
> *t*ʻ*ā/γ*ᴀ́*t/nā* "he drinks"

Examples of third persons with -ᴀ- followed by an inorganic consonant are:

> *dȧ̆/n*ᴀ*t/t*ʻᴀ̀*c* "he went to bed" (-*t*- is not third modal; cf. second person singular *dā/nı̇̆/t*ʻᴀ*c*)
>
> *t*ʻ*é/*ᴀ*n/γ*ᴀ*l/l*ᴀ*ł* "he is sinking in the water" (-*l*- is not third modal; cf. second person singular *t*ʻ*é/*ᴀ*n/γī/l*ᴀ*ł*)

First modal *n*-, reduced from *ne*-, however, has in several cases been found without following inorganic vowel and consonant.

In such cases it closes the preceding syllable, which may even belong to another word. Examples are:

> *dȯ/dAt 'An/t!e* "not-anywhere there-is" (cf. Kato *ąn/t'ē* "it is;" Hupa *ûn/ṯe* "there is")
>
> *łán/dō* "nine" (really *ła n/dō* "one is-lacking"); *nā/xÁn/dō* "eight" (reduced from *nȧ/xi n/dō* "two are-lacking") (cf. Kato *n/dōᵋ/bûñ* "it will not be," but also *nût/dōᵋ* "all gone")
>
> *cíc/mAnèn/dá'* (=*ci̇ c/mAnè n/da'*) "I my-house is" (cf. Chipewyan *ne/da* "she sat")

If the verb form consists, properly speaking, of the stem alone, without prefix of any kind, an inorganic A- completed by a consonant that depends for its form on the first consonant of the stem is prefixed for the third person:

> *As/sé/t'e* "he must cry" (<**se/t'e*; cf. *dȯ/As/se* "I'm not crying" <**Ac/se*)
>
> *dō/wa/Al/lê'* "he will become" (<**lê*; *dō/wa* is adverb not influencing form of verb proper. That *-l-* is here no third modal element is shown by forms like Hupa *ō/le* "let him become")

This A- at the beginning of a third personal form appears also when the verb begins with a third modal element:

> *Al/Áz* "he sneezes"

In this respect Chasta Costa differs from Kato, which need have nothing preceding the stem; with *As/se* compare Kato *tce'* "he cried."

In the third person of definite tenses with second modal γ- or *n*- prefix this element is followed by -ī, in case there is no third modal prefix present. This goes back, without doubt, to nasalized *-i-* or -A-, in turn reduced from original *-iŋ-* (or -Aŋ-). This nasal element, characteristic of definite third personal forms (except such as have θ-, Athabascan *s*-, as second modal prefix) is found also in Hupa (*-iñ-*), Kato (*-ûn-*), and Chipewyan (*-n-*, *-in-*). Examples are:

t'e/nī/lat "he drowns" (cf. Kato *tc'n/nûl/lat* "it floated there," *nûl-* assimilated from *nûn-*; *t'e/nī/lat* also "you drown")

γī/dac "he dances" (cf. Kato *tc'/gûn/dac/kwañ* "he had danced")

yā/γī/t!a "it flies" (cf. Hupa *na/win/tau* "it will settle down;" *yā/γī/t!a* also "it flies")

dīⁱ/s'at' "it pains" (*dīⁱ-<*diη-*, contracted[51] from **de/-γiη-*; cf. Hupa *dū/win/tcat* "it got sick")

Rather hard to understand is:

t'é/ᴀn/γᴀl/lᴀt "he is sinking in the water"

One would have expected *-γī-*, not *-γᴀl-* (as seen above, *-l-* is not third modal, but inorganic). Is *γᴀ-* reduced from first modal *γe-*, this form being indefinite in tense?

In Hupa this *-iñ-* does not seem to be found before third modal prefixes; in Chipewyan *-n-* (*-in-*) may, however, occur before *-ł-* and, as inferred from Father Legoff's Montagnais paradigms, also *-l-*. As for Chasta Costa, what examples are available on this point show that *-i-* does not occur before *-l-* (e. g. *yā/γᴀ́l/gᴀθ* "he climbs"). For *ł-* verbs I have no safe example. Before *-t-* it seems that *-i-* is present in some cases, not in others:

tc!ō/γít/siʟ/la "he pointed with his finger"

but, without *-i-*:

na/da/γᴀ́t/t!ō "he is bathing"

On the whole, it seems possible that Athabascan *-ᴀη-* (or *-ᴀn-*) was originally a more freely movable element than it has

---

[51] Parallel in form to Hupa verbs belonging to Class I, Conjugation 1 D, in which prefixed first modal *d-* or deictic *kʸ!-* contracts with *-iη*, *w-* (Athabascan *γ-*) being lost. See Goddard, *op. cit.*, p. 113.

become in e. g. Hupa, being required by certain verbs in their definite tenses, but not by others. This is suggested also by Father Legoff's Montagnais paradigms.

THIRD MODAL PREFIXES. There are three of these: *-ł-*, *-l-*, and *-t-*; they always complete a syllable immediately before the stem. *-ł-* is characteristic of many verbs which are either transitive or, at any rate, imply activity directed outward; in some cases, however, this significance is not obvious. As we have seen, this *-ł-* becomes *-l-* in the first and second persons plural. Examples of *-ł-*(*-L-*) are:

θícł/t'āł "I kicked him"
tθ!Aθ/dà cAł nā/θił/sī "story to-me you-told, made"
nécł/ī "I'm looking at him"
nåł/dè "he washes (something)"
nał/L!ò "he writes"
tc!Ał/t!ō "he sucks"
yů/wīs dAł/nī "he whistles;" *yů/wīs dAcł/nī* "I whistle"[52]
xwAn/né/θiL/ya "you win"

If nothing precedes this element, it seems (unlike *-l-*) to begin its word without preceding inorganic *A-*:

dō/wa/ł/t'át/nAł "they will be broken" (*dō/wa* is merely proclitic)
ł/t'ī "he is important"

Verbs in *-l-* are regularly intransitive; they denote states of mind or bodily activities that may be thought of as self-contained, not directed outwards. A reflexive meaning is sometimes apparent. After first person subjective *-c-* (*-s-*) it always appears as *-ł-*. Hence the first person singular, the first person plural, and the second person plural of *-ł-* verbs and *l-* verbs are always alike (but contrast *θicł-*<**sAcł-* with *sAsł*<**sAcl-*). As *-l-*, when standing after *s*, becomes *-ł-* also in the third person, the second person singular alone remains

[52] This verb is irregular, inasmuch as *-ł-* does not occur in the second person singular: *yů/wīs dī/nī* "you whistle."

as an infallible criterion of whether a verb belongs to the *ł*-class or *l*- class. Examples of *-l-* are:

ya/dᴀ́l/yᴀc "he is ashamed"
xwᴀ́cʟ/ī "I believe;" *xwil/ị/ha* "do you expect?"
t'ᴀ́l/dᴀc "he runs"
yā/γᴀ́l/gᴀθ "he climbs"
nȧ/dᴀl/dè "he washed himself"
ᴀl/ᴀ́z "he sneezes"
t'ᴀ́l/xwᴀθ "he coughs"
na/xᴀt/da/γᴀ́l/eł "they are bathing"
nā/xwᴀ́l/ye "he plays"
nā/dᴀ́l/nic "he works"
tc!ásʟ/se "he cries;" *tc!ā/θíl/se* "you cry"
tc!ácʟ/se/t'e "I'll cry;" *tc!ȧl/se/t'e* "you'll cry"
hȯ/γᴀcʟ/ī "I stop, cease;" *hȯ/il/ī* "stop!"

Verbs in *-t-* are also intransitive. Examples are:

t'ā/γít/nā "you drink"
ye/γát/ne/la "he bit (it)"
tc!ō/γít/siʟ/la "he pointed with his finger"
q!wᴀ́t/daθt/gᴀ̀c "it lies thrown down on top, table-cloth"
γᴀ́ct/lò "I laugh" (*-t/lō* may, however, represent original Athabascan *-dlō* "to laugh")
ya/da/γít/dja "we are ashamed"

There may be a passive significance in:

q!wᴀ́t/tc!ᴀt/dja "whereon it is eaten, table"

With iterative *na-*:

na/γȧ/θᴀθt/xwī "I vomit"

Verb Stems. The stems that have been determined for Chasta Costa are:

-'ā,-'a "to have position, to be" (cf. Hupa *-ai, -a*; Kato *-'ai'*, *-'a'*): *θ/'ā/la* "(one table) was"

-*'ᴀc* "to bring" (cf. Hupa *-an*, *-ûñ*, *-auw̲* "to transport round objects"; Kato *-ʿq̨ñ*, *-ʿq̨c*): *γᴀn/na/'ᴀ́c* "he will bring it"

-*'ᴀn* "to bring to a halt, stop" (perhaps another form of preceding stem): *nā/nɨ/ᴀn* "stop him!"

-*ᴀz* "to sneeze": *ᴀcʟ/ᴀ́z* "I sneeze"

-*ał* "to come" (cf. Chipewyan *-ʿas*, *-ʿaz*, *-ʿais* "to travel, used of two persons only"?) *an/γɨ/'ał* "come on!"

-*êł*, *-eł* "to bathe (plur. subject)" (cf. Chipewyan *-el*, *-eʟ*, *-ūʟ* "to move on the surface of water"): *na/da/γíl/êł* "we are bathing"

-*'ī* "to see, look at" (cf. Hupa *-en*, *-iñ*; Kato *-ʿīñʿ* "to look"): *γe/θíc/ī* "I saw him"

-*ī* "to stop, cease" (cf. Hupa *-en*, *-iñ* "to do, to act, to deport one's self"?): *hő/γᴀcʟ/ī* "I stop (laughing)"

-*ī* "to believe, expect": *xwᴀ́cʟ/ī* "I believe"

-*ya*, *-yᴀc*, *-yic* "to go, come" (cf. Hupa *-yai*, *-ya*, *-yauw̲*; Kato *-yai*, *-ya*, *-yac*): *t'e/θíc/ya* "I go;" *t'ᴀc/yᴀ́c/t'e* "I must go"

-*ya* "to eat" (cf. Hupa *-yan*, *-yûñ*, *-yauw̲*; Kato *-yanʿ* *-yīlʿ*): *tc!ᴀγ/γe/θíc/ya* "I eat;" *q!wᴀ́t/tc!ᴀt/dja*(<*-t/ya*) "whereon one eats, table"

-*ya* "to win" (cf. Kato *-yan*, "Kato Texts," p. 146, l. 13; not listed in "Elements of the Kato Language"): *xwᴀn/né/θiʟ/ya* "you win"

-*yan* "to upset" (cf. Kato *-yañ* "to clear off"?): *dō/wá/ᴀn/-nā/yan/nᴀł* "he will upset them"

-*ya*, *-yᴀc* "to be ashamed" (cf. Kato *-yañ* "to be ashamed"): *ya/dᴀ́l/yᴀc* "he is ashamed;" *ya/da/γít/dja* (<*-t/ya*) "we are ashamed"

-*ye* "to play" (cf. Hupa *-ye* "to dance"): *nā/xwᴀ́l/ye* "he plays"

-*lał* "to sleep" (cf. Hupa *-lal*, *-laʟ*; Kato *-lal*, *-lq̨ʟ*): *t'éθ/-lał/la* "he's been sleeping"

-*lᴀł* "to sink in water;" *-lat* "to drown" (cf. Hupa *-lat*,

-la "to float"): *t'é/An/γAc/lAł* "I am sinking;" *t'e/-níc/lat* "I drown"

-lê "to become" (cf. Hupa *-len, -liñ, -lū, -le*; Kato *-liñ*ᵋ, *-le*): *dō/wa/Al/lê'* "it will become"

-lec "to wager, bet": *né/tc!ūc/lec* "I'll bet you"

-lec "to smoke": *mAł/t'é/tc!At/ts!Al/léc* "wherewith it is smoked"

-lō "to laugh, smile" (cf. Chipewyan *-dlō, -dlōk'*): *γít/lō* "laugh!"

-L!ō "to write" (cf. Hupa *-Lōn, -Lō, -Lōw, -Loi* "to make baskets, to twine in basket-making;" Kato *-Lōi, -Lō, -Lōn*): *nał/L!ö* "he writes"

-nā "to drink" (cf. Hupa *-nan, -nûñ*; Kato *-nąn*): *t'ā/-γÁct/nā* "I drink"

-nā "to lie" (cf. Kato *nōL/tin/na*ᵋ "were left"?): *q!wÁt/dasL/nà* "it was lying on it"

-ne "to bite, seize with one's teeth": *ye/γát/ne/la* "he bit it"

-nī, -n "to make a sound, to say" (cf. Hupa *-ne, -n* "to speak, to make a sound;" Kato *-nī, -ne, -n, -nec, -nīL*): *yú/wīs dAł/nī* "he whistles;" *á/djAn* "he says"

-nic "to work": *nā/dÁl/nic* "he works" (cf. Montagnais *-ni* "exprime l'action des mains"[53]

-θAł "to wash oneself (plur. subject)" (cf. Hupa *-sel, -seL* "to be or to become warm;" Kato *-sīl* "to steam," *-sûl, -sûL* "to be warm"): *tc!At/t'ít/θAł* "we wash ourselves"

-θeł "to throw": *yā/γí/θeł* "you threw"

-se "to cry" (cf. Hupa *-tcwū, -tcwe* "to cry, to weep;" Kato *-tceG, -tce'*): *tc!ásL/se* "he cries"

-sī "to cause" (cf. Hupa *-tcwen, -tcwiñ, -tcwe* "to make, to arrange, to cause;" Kato *-tcin, -tcī, -tcīL*): *nácł/sī* "I cause"

-sił "to point with one's finger": *tc!ō/γít/siL/la* "he pointed with his finger"

---

[53] Father L. Legoff, "Grammaire de la Langue Montagnaise," p. 139.

-da', *-dā* "to sit, stay" (cf. Hupa *-dai*, *-da*; Kato *-da*, *-dai*): *dā/θi/dā* "you are sitting"

-dᴀc "to run" (cf. Hupa *-dal*, *-daʟ*, *-dauw̲* "to pass along, to go, to come;" Kato *-dac* "to travel"): *t'ᴀl/dᴀc* "he runs"

-dac "to dance" (cf. Kato *-dac* "to dance"): *ni/dac* "you dance"

-de "to wash (sing. subject)" (cf. Kato *-deɢ*, *-de'*): *nȧ/dᴀl/dè* "he washed himself"

-t'āł "to kick" (cf. Hupa *-taʟ*, *-tûl*, *-tûʟ*, *-tal* "to step, to kick;" Kato *-tal'*, *-tąʟ*): *θícł/t'āł* "I kicked him"

-t'ᴀc "to lie down, go to bed" (cf. Hupa *-ten*, *-tiñ*, *-tūw̲* "to lie down;" Kato *-tin*, *-tûc*): *dȧ/nᴀc/t'ᴀ̀c* "I go to bed"

-t'at "to break, go to pieces" (cf. Chipewyan *-taʟ*, *-tûl* "to break"): *dō/wa/ł/t'át/nᴀł* "they will be broken"

-t'e "to want" (cf. Hupa *-te* "to look for, to search after"?): *dȯ/ucʟ/t'e* "I do not want;" *dé/ucʟ/t'e* "what I want"

-t'ī "to be, make valuable" (cf. Carrier *tîł/thî* "thou makest him valuable, treatest him as important"): *ł/t'i γᴀn/na/'à* "he brags"

-t!a "to fly" (cf. Hupa *-t̯au*; Kato *-t'aɢ*, *-t'a'*): *dō/yác/t!a* "I won't fly"

-t!e "to be of (that) sort" (cf. Hupa *-t̯e*; Kato *-t'e*): *dȯ/dᴀt 'ᴀn/t!e* "there is not anywhere (one like him)"

-t!ō "to swim, bathe (sing. subject)": *nac/t!ȯ* "I swim, bathe"

-t!ō "to suck" (cf. Kato *-t'ōt*): *tc!ᴀ́ł/t!ō* "he sucks"

-tθ!i "to sit (plur. subject)" (cf. Hupa *-tse*; Chipewyan *-θ'ī*): *dā/de/θíl/tθ!i* "we are sitting"

-ts!at "to hurt, pain (intr.)" (cf. Hupa *-tcat*, *-tca* "to be sick, to become ill"): *dí'/s'at'* "(my eyes) hurt"

-γa "to go about, live" (cf. Hupa *-wai*, *-wa* "to go, to go about;" Kato *-ga*, *-gai*): *nȧ/γa* "he goes about, lives"

-xe "to paddle" (cf. Hupa *-xen*, *-xūw̲* "to float, used only of plural objects;" Kato *-ke'* "to bathe (plural only);"

Chipewyan *-kĩ* "to paddle a canoe, to travel by canoe"): *nác/xe* "I paddle"

-xwʌθ "to cough" (cf. Kato *kōs* "cough," as noun; Carrier *xwœs*): *t'ʌ́l/xwʌθ* "he coughs"

-xwī "to vomit" (cf. Carrier *khu* "vomiting," as noun): *na/γả/θʌθt/xwị* "I vomit"

-gʌθ "to climb" (cf. Hupa *-kas* "to throw"): *yā/γʌ́l/gʌθ* "he climbs"

-gʌc "to throw"? (cf. Hupa *-kas* "to throw"): *q!wʌ́t/daθt/-gʌ̀c* "it lies thrown down on top, table-cloth"

It will be observed that several verb stems are restricted in their use as regards number of subject (or object). This trait is characteristic of Athabascan, as also of other American linguistic stocks.

Definite and Indefinite Tenses. My material on Chasta Costa is not full enough to enable me to give a satisfactory idea of its tense-mode system. It is clear, however, that absolute time (present, past, future) is quite subordinate to whether activities are thought of as taking place at some definite time (generally present or past) or are more indefinite as to time occurrence. Indefinite forms are apt to be used for general statements that apply irrespective of any particular time, for future acts, for negative (particularly negative future) acts, and regularly for imperative and prohibitive forms. The contrast between definite and indefinite present forms comes out in:

definite: *ná/da/γʌct/t!ǒ* "I bathe" (i. e. am now engaged in bathing)
indefinite: *cʌ́ł/q!we na/dʌct/t!ō* "I'm used to bathing" (here bathing is not restricted as to time)

definite: *tc!ā/sʌ́sʟ/se* "I cry"
indefinite: *t'wị/dʌn ʌs/se* "I always cry"

definite: *γéθt/lō* "he breaks into laughter" (i. e. laughs at one particular point of time)
indefinite: *γát/lō* "he laughs"

definite: *xAt/t'é/laɫ/la* "they have been sleeping" (may be said of them at moment of waking up)
indefinite: *xAt/t'Al/laɫ* "they sleep"

Futures, as we shall see, are explicitly rendered by suffixing *-t'e* to present (generally indefinite) forms; but simple indefinite forms, particularly with adverbs pointing to future time, may often be used as futures in contrast to definite present forms. Examples are:

definite: *na/da/γíl/êɫ* "we are bathing"
indefinite: *nā/díl/eɫ* "we'll bathe"

definite *tθ!Áθ/dà cAɫ na/θīɫ/sī* "story to-me you-told"
indefinite: *xún/dè tθ!Aθ/dā nAɫ nácɫ/sī* "tomorrow story to-you I-tell"

definite: *n/γe/θic/ī* "I saw you"
indefinite: *xAL/ts!i/dAn dō/wan/γAc/ī* "this-evening I'll-see-you"

definite: *t'e/θíc/ya* "I go"
indefinite: *xun/dé t'ac/yAc* "tomorrow I'll-go"

Negative presents or futures are regularly expressed by prefixing *dō* "not" to indefinite forms; when more explicitly future, *-t'e* is suffixed to them. Examples of indefinite forms preceded by *dō* are:

definite: *tc!ac yā/γi/t!a* "bird is-flying"
indefinite: *dō/yȧ/t!a* "he won't fly"

definite: *na/γȧ/θAθt/xwi* "I vomit"
indefinite: *dō/na/γÁct/xwī* "I do not vomit"

definite: *tc!ā/sÁsL/se* "I cry;" *tc!ā/θíl/se* "you cry"
indefinite: *dȯ/As/se* "I'm not crying;" *dȯ/ī/se* "you're not crying"

definite: *γe/θic/ī* "I saw him;" *c/γe/θi/ī* "you saw me"
indefinite: *dō/γÁc/ī* "I didn't see him;" *dō/lȧ/c/γī/ī* "you didn't see me"

definite: *t'e/θíc/ya* "I go;" *t'éθ/ya* "he goes"
indefinite: *dō/t'Ác/yic* "I'll not go;" *dō/t'Ác* "he won't go" (<**t'A/yAc*)

Imperatives are simply second person subjective indefinite forms. Examples are:

γi̇/ī "see him!" *c/γi̇/ī* "see me!"
nél/ī "look at him!" (identical with indefinite present: *nél/ī* "you're looking at him"); *ne/cíl/ī* "look at me!"
nā/ni̇/ʌn "stop him!"

Prohibitives are simply imperative forms preceded by *ła*:

ła/γi̇/ī "don't see him!"

First person plural indefinite forms may have hortatory significance:

nā/xwíl/ye "let us play!"

As regards form, definite tenses are primarily distinguished from indefinite tenses by the presence of second modal prefixes in the former, often also by the appearance of the first modal prefixes in a fuller form than in the latter; the presence of *-ī-* or *-i-* in certain third person definite forms may also be recalled. It seems, further, that certain adverbial prefixes which have a short vowel (even though in an open syllable) in definite forms lengthen it in corresponding indefinite forms:

definite: *ná/da/γʌct/t!ȱ* "I bathe;" *na/da/γít/t!ō* "you bathe;" *na/da/γʌ́t/t!ō* "he's bathing"
indefinite: *nā/dʌct/t!ȱ˙/t'e* "I'll bathe;" *nā/dít/t!ō/t'e* "you'll bathe;" *nā/dʌ́t/t!ō/t'e* "he'll bathe"

definite: *na/da/γíl/êł* "we are bathing;" *na/da/γȱl/êł* "ye are bathing;" *na/xʌt/da/γʌ́l/eł* "they are bathing"
indefinite: *nā/díl/eł* "we'll bathe;" *nā/dȱl/eł* "ye will bathe;" *nā/xʌt/dʌ́l/eł* "they'll bathe"

definite: *tc!a/γǡ/θil/se* "we cry;" *tc!a/γǡ/θōl/se* "ye cry"
indefinite: *tc!ā/γál/se* "we'll cry;" *tc!ā/γǡl/se/t'e* "ye will cry"

These changes of quantity, however, are doubtless only secondarily connected with change of tense, as indicated, e. g., by *tc!ā-* in definite singular forms: *tc!ā/sᴀ́sʟ/se* "I cry;" *tc!ā/-θíl/se/ha* "do you cry?" It is very likely that we are dealing here primarily with considerations of syllabic and quantitative rhythm or balance.[54]

In Hupa Goddard has exhaustively shown that verb stems often assume different forms for different tenses and modes. This is very likely also true to a considerable extent of Chasta Costa, but I have but little material bearing on this point. A quantitative change is found in:

definite *-êł*: *na/da/γíl/êł* "we are bathing"
indefinite *-eł*: *nā/díl/eł* "we'll bathe"

-c characterizes indefinite forms in:

definite *-ya*: *tʻe/θíc/ya* "I go;" *tʻe/θɨ́/ya* "you go"
indefinite *-yᴀc*: *tʻᴀc/yᴀ́c/tʻe* "I must go;" *tʻī/yᴀ́c/tʻe* "you must go"
negative indefinite *-yic*: *dō/tʻᴀ́c/yic* "I'll not go;" *łá/tʻī/-yic* "don't go!"

definite *-ya*: *ya/da/γít/dja*(<*-t/ya*) "we are ashamed"
indefinite *-yᴀc*: *ya/dᴀ́cł/yᴀc* "I am ashamed"

Pronominal Objects. Pronominal objects are regularly prefixed to the verb. They come before deictic and first modal elements, but after adverbial prefixes. Thus, while not as thoroughly immersed in the verb form as the subjective pronominal elements, they cannot well be considered apart from it. The third person singular object is not designated. In form the objective elements are, on the whole, identical with the possessive pronominal prefixes of the noun. They are:

Singular	1.	*c-*	Plural	1.	*nō-*
	2.	*n-*, *ne-*		2.	*nō-*
	3.	—		3.	*xō-*

[54] Hardly stress accent as such. I cannot help feeling that such rhythmic phenomena will turn out to be of fundamental importance for Athabascan generally.

"He—them" or "they—them" is expressed by means of *xī-*. *c-* and *n-*, when standing at the beginning of a verb form, take no inorganic *A-* before them (contrast subjective *Ac-*).

The definite forms of *γéθ/ī* "he saw him" with combined pronominal subject and object are:

With first person singular object:

Sing. 2.	*c/γe/θi̇/ī* "you saw me"	Plural 2.	*c/γe/θȱ/ī*
3.	*c/γéθ/ī*	3.	*c/xA/γéθ/ī*

With second person singular object:

Sing. 1.	*n/γe/θi̇c/ī* "I saw you"	Plural 1.	*n/γe/θít/ī*
3.	*n/γéθ/ī*	3.	*n/xA/γéθ/ī*

With first person plural object:

Sing. 2.	*nō/γe/θȱ/ī* "you saw us"	Plural 2.	*nō/γé/θō/ī*
3.	*nō/γéθ/ī*	3.	*nō/xA/γéθ/ī*

For *nō/γe/θȱ/ī* "you saw us" one would have expected **nō/-γe/θī/ī*. It seems that "ye saw us" has been extended in its usage to embrace also "you (sing.) saw us." It may indeed be that my data on this point rest on a misunderstanding, but there seems to be something analogous in Hupa. "You (sing.) are picking us up" would be expected in Hupa to be **yûn/nō/-hil/lūw̱* (*hil-* assimilated from *hiñ-*). Instead of this form, however, Goddard lists *yûn/nō/hōl/lūw̱*, which is not identical with but seems, as regards its second *ō-* vowel, to have been influenced by *yûn/nō/hō/lūw̱* "ye are picking us up."[55]

With second person plural object:

Sing. 1.	*nō/γe/θi̇c/ī* "I saw you (pl.)"	Plural 1.	*nō/γe/θít/ī*
3.	*nō/γéθ/ī/la*	3.	*nō/xA/γéθ/ī/la*

[55] Goddard, *op. cit.*, p. 186.

With third person singular object:

Sing.	1.	*γe/θí̇c/ī* "I saw him"	Plural	1.	*γe/θít/ī*
	2.	*γe/θi̇/ī*		2.	*γe/θȯ/ī*
	3.	*γéθ/ī*		3.	*xī/γéθ/ī*

With third person plural object:

Sing.	1.	*xō/γé/θīc/ī* "I saw them"	Plural	1.	*xō/γé/θit/ī* (heard also as *xō/we-*)
	2.	*γe/θȯ/ī*		2.	*xō/γé/θō/ī*
	3.	*xī/dᴀ/γéθ/ī*		3.	*xī/γéθ/ī/la*

Here again, one would have expected **xō/γe/θi̇/ī* for "you (sing.) saw them." As it is, "you (pl.) saw him" seems to be used also for "you (sing.) saw them," both forms being logically parallel in that both involve a second person—third person relation, only one of the two persons, however, being plural. Objective forms of indefinite tenses of this verb are:

With first person singular object:

dō/wa/c/γī/i̇^{i}*/t'e* "you'll see me"
dō/lȧ/c/γī/ī "you didn't see me"
c/γi̇/ī "see me!"
c/γa/i̇^{i}*/t'ē* "he'll see me"

With second person singular object:

dō/wa/n/γᴀ́c/ī "I'll see you"

With third person singular object:

dō/wa/γᴀ́c/ī "I'll see him"
dō/γᴀ́c/ī "I didn't see him"
dō/γᴀ́c/ī/t'e "I won't see him"
dō/wa/γī/i̇/t'e "you'll see him"
γi̇/ī "see him!"
ła/γi̇/ī "don't see him!"

Objective forms of indefinite tenses of *ne-ł-'ī* "to look at" are:

With first person singular object:

ne/cíł/ī "look at me!"
ne/cᴀ́ł/ī "he looks at me"

With third person singular object:

> *nécł/ī* "I'm looking at him"
> *dō/nécł/ī* "I'm not looking at him"
> *néł/ī* "you're looking at him;" "look at him!"
> *nél/ī* "let's look at him!"
> *ne/xȯ/ōl/ī* "you (plur.) look at him"

This last form may, likely enough, have been mistranslated for "you (plur.) look at them" (cf. *xō/γé/θō/ī* above).
Other forms with first person singular object are:

> *cᴀ́sł/sī* "he lets me, causes me to"
> *cᴀsł/t'ȧł* "he kicked me"

With second person singular object:

> *né/tc!ūc/lec* "I'll bet you"

Passives. As in Hupa, pronominal subjects of passive verbs are objective in form. From *ne-ł-'ī* are formed:

nés/ts!ᴀł/ī "I am seen"	*ne/nȯ/ts!ᴀł/ī* "we are seen"
nén/ts!ᴀł/ī "you are seen"	*ne/nȯ/ts!ᴀł/ī* "ye are seen"
nê'/ts!ᴀł/ī "he is seen"	*ne/xȯ/ts!ᴀł/ī* "they are seen"

ts!ᴀł-, which appears in these forms, probably contains third modal *-ł-* preceded by deictic *ts!-* implying indefiniteness of logical subject: "man sieht mich." Apparently connected with this *ts!ᴀł-* is *ts!ᴀl-* in:

> *mᴀł/t'é/tc!ᴀt/ts!ᴀl/lec* "wherewith it is smoked, smoking utensils"

Verbal Suffixes. A number of enclitic elements of temporal or modal significance are found rather loosely suffixed to verb forms. These, so far as illustrated in our material, are:

-t'e future particle (cf. Hupa *-te*, *-teʟ*; Kato *-teʟ*, *-tē/le*):

> *ᴀcʟ/ᴀ́z/t'e* "I shall sneeze"
> *t'ᴀc/lát/t'e* "I shall sleep"
> *nā/dᴀct/t!ȯ'/t'e* "I shall bathe"
> *nécł/ī/t'e* "I'll look at him"
> *dō/γᴀ́c/ī/t'e* "I won't see him"

nā/dAcL/nic/t'e "I shall work"
dō/nȧ/dAcL/nic/t'e "I shall not work"
tc!ácL/se/t'e "I shall cry"
dō/Ás/se/t'e "I'll not cry"
tc!ȧl/se/t'e "you will cry"

-t'e seems to imply obligation to some extent, as well as simple futurity, as is shown by its translation as "must" in some cases:

As/sé/t'e "he must cry"
t'Ac/yÁc/t'e "I must go"
t'ī/yÁc/t'e "you must go"

All forms with suffixed *-t'e*, it will be noticed, are indefinite; none has been found that is definite.

-nAł seems to be used for future acts:

dō/wá/An/nā/yan/nAł "he will upset them"
dō/wa/ł/t'át/nAł "they will be broken, go to pieces"

-ha, *-hā* interrogative:

nā/xwíl/ye/ha "are you playing?"
t'e/θȯ/lał/ha "have ye been sleeping?"
nō/γe/θȯ/ī/ha "did you see us?"
neł/i̇/ha "did you look at him?"
tc!ā/θíl/se/ha "did you cry?"
dȯ/ō/se/ha "are ye not crying?"
As/sé/t'e/ha "will he cry?"
tc!ā/γȧl/se/t'e/ha "will ye cry?"
t'ā/γít/nā/hā "do you drink?"

ha seems to both precede and follow in:

ha/xwil/i̇/ha "do you expect?"

-la probably inferential (cf. Hupa *-xō/lan*, *-xō/lûñ*):

t'e/θÁθ/lał/la "I've been sleeping" (said on waking up)
Lȧθ/ā/la "there was one (table)"
txAs/xé/la "(evidently) rich"

Probably also in:

dō/wɨ/la "of course"

-la seems also to be used of simple narrative in past time, with very weak, if any, inferential force:

tc!ō/γít/siʟ/la "he pointed with his finger"
ye/γát/ne/la "he bit it"
nᴀn/ṇáθ/yā/la "he went around it"
nō/γéθ/ī/la "he saw you (plur.)" (cf. *nō/γéθ/ī* "he saw us")
nō/xᴀ/γéθ/ī/la "they saw you (plur.)" (cf. *nō/xᴀ/γéθ/ī* "they saw us")
xī/γéθ/ī/la "they saw them" (cf. *xī/γéθ/ī* "they saw him")

I do not know whether the contrasts in person and number found in the last three pairs of forms are real or only apparent.

-le of unknown significance

nā/xōl/yé/le "you (plur.) play"

Syntactic Combination of Verbs. Two verb forms sometimes combine syntactically, one depending on the other. The second verb is subordinate to the first in:

dṓ/ucʟ/t'e nā/xwᴀcʟ/ye "I-do-not-want I-play," i. e. "I don't want to play"
hṓ/γᴀcʟ/ī γᴀct/lō "I-stop I-laugh," i. e. "I stop laughing"
hṓ/il/ī γit/lō "stop laugh!" i. e. "stop laughing!"
ha/xwil/ɨ/ha γᴀ́n/na/ᴀ́c "do-you-expect he-will bring?"

It seems that sometimes the first verb, which is then a third personal form, acts as a sort of complementary infinitive to the second:

yā/γɨ/t!a θicł/sī "he-flies I-make-him," i. e. "I let him fly"
yā/γɨ/t!a cᴀsł/sī "he-flies he makes-me," i. e. "he lets me fly"
ł/t'ɨ γᴀn/na/'à "he-is-important he-has-for(?)," i. e. "he brags about him"

TEXT: THE GOOD DOG.[56]

ł/t'ī́[57]	γAn/na/'à[58]	xā́/dAt[59]	lī/tc!é.[60]	dṓ/dAt[61]
Make important	he has	his own	dog.	"Nowhere
'An/t!e[62]	nā́/γa[63]	ā́/djAn.[64]	dé/ucL/t'e[65]	hī́/t!i[66]
is like him	moves about,"	he says.	"What I want	that thing

---

[56] Wolverton Orton claimed not to know any regular Chasta Costa myth texts. The following, which is merely an English joke anecdote taken from a popular periodical that happened to be lying about and translated into Chasta Costa by Mr. Orton, will at least serve to give some idea of Chasta Costa word order and sentence construction.

[57] *ł-*, third modal element. *-t'ī*, verb stem. Cf. Carrier *tîl/thî* "thou makest him valuable, treatest him as important."

[58] *γAn-* and *na-*, adverbial prefixes. *-'a*, verb stem. For *na/'a-* "to have," cf. Hupa *nañ/a/te* "you will have." "He has his dog made valuable, treated as important," i. e., "he brags about his dog." Indefinite tense, because statement is general and does not refer to any one point of time.

[59] *x-*, third personal pronominal element. *-ā/dAt*, reflexive possessive element.

[60] Possessed form of *łī* "dog." Observe change of *ł-* to *l-*, and suffixing of *-tc!e*. Cf. Hupa *-liñ/k(y!)e;* Chipewyan *Lin/k'e*.

[61] *dō*, negative adverb. *-dAt*, postpositive element.

[62] *'A-*, reduced from *'a-*, prefix used with verbs of saying, doing, and being. It is probably equivalent to indefinite demonstrative: "(there is of) that (kind)." *-n-*, first modal element. *-t!e*, verb stem. Cf. Hupa *ûn/te* "there is;" Kato *qn/t'ē* "it is;" Chipewyan *an/t'e/hī/k'e* "it was." Indefinite tense, because statement is general.

[63] *nā-*, adverbial prefix. *-γa*, verb stem. "Moves about," i. e., "is living, is to be found": "there is no (dog) like him anywhere." Cf. Hupa *na/wa* "they were there;" Kato *na/ga/kwqn* "he had walked;" Navaho *na/Ga*, i. e., *na/γa*, "he is going about" (quoted from Goddard, Analysis of Cold Lake Dialect, Chipewyan). Indefinite tense; general statement.

[64] *ā-*, prefix used with verb of saying; see note 62. *dj-*, third personal deictic prefix; or perhaps *djA-* = **dyA-*, reduced from **dye-*, first modal prefix *d-* and third person deictic prefix *ye-*. *-n*, verb stem. Probably definite in tense, though it shows no second modal prefix; cf. Hupa present definite third singular *a/den*.

[65] *de*, apparently relative in force. *u-*, adverbial prefix. *-c-*, first person singular subjective element. *-L-*, third modal prefix. *-t'e*, verb stem. Indefinite tense; general statement.

[66] *hī*, demonstrative stem. *-t!i*, suffix applying, it would seem, to things. Perhaps *hī/t!i* is assimilated from **hī/t!a;* for *-t!a*, cf. Chipewyan *t!a* "that; often used to point out one of several persons or things characterized by a descriptive phrase or clause."

s/ts!An/na/'Ác[67]	ał/dAc/ní/dAn.[68]	dő	t'wī/dè[69]	Lá	ā/djAn.
to me he brings	when I tell him."	"Not	everything,"	one	says.

łí/t!i/nī[70]	mAn/mé/q!e[71]	t'/γí/ī.[72]	xat	q!wÁt/tc!At/djà[73]
Dog-owner	around in house	he looked around.	Then	table

Lá́θ/ā/la[74]	mAn/mé[75]	wAs/xé	q!wÁt/daθt/gÀc[76]	nāθ/L!ő[77]
one there was	in house.	Good	table-cloth,	paper

hī	q!wÁt/dasL/nà[78]	ī/γí/tc'u[79]	mAł/t'é/tc!At/ts!Al/léc.[80]
that	was lying thereon,	that	wherewith it is smoked.

---

[67] *s-*, assimilated from *c-*, objective (or possessive) first person singular pronominal element. *-ts!An*, postposition. *na-*, adverbial prefix. *-'Ac*, verb stem. Cf. Hupa *dō/xō/liñ/na/ta/auw* "he won't carry." Indefinite tense; general statement.

[68] *a-*, as in notes 62 and 64. *-ł-*, postposition; refers to implied third person indirect object of verb. *-d-*, first modal prefix. *-c-*, as in note 65. *-nī*, verb stem. *-dAn*, postposition; here used to subordinate verb. Cf. Hupa *ûn/niL/dūw/ne* "I am telling you." Indefinite tense; general statement.

[69] *t'wī*, pronominal stem denoting totality. *-de*, indefinite demonstrative stem.

[70] *łī* "dog." *-tli/nī* "one who has;" evidently contains common Athabascan suffix *-n*, *-nī* "person."

[71] *mAn* "house." *-me/q!e*, compound postposition.

[72] *t'-*, first modal prefix reduced from *t'e-*. *γī-*, first modal prefix *γ-* reduced from *γe-*, *-ī-* remaining unexplained. *-ī*, verb stem. According to this analysis, *t'/γī/ī* is indefinite in tense; this seems hard to understand, as it refers to one act in past time. Another analysis seems more likely: *t'-*, instead of or misheard for *t'e-*, form regularly used in definite tenses; *γ-*, second modal prefix; *-ī-*, definite third person ending for *γ-* verbs. Cf. Hupa *tcit/te/we/iñ/il* "he looked about as he went along."

[73] *q!wAt-*, postposition "upon" used as adverbial prefix. *tc!-*, deictic prefix here indicating indefiniteness of object. *-t-*, third modal prefix presumably with passive force. *-dja*, from *-ya* after *-t-*, verb stem "to eat." "It is eaten thereon," i. e., "table."

[74] *Lā*, numeral "one," to which verb proper, *θ/ā/la*, is attached. *θ-*, second modal prefix. *ā-*, verb stem. *-la*, verb suffix. Definite past tense, because referring to definite point of time in narrative. Cf. Chipewyan *ϑe/'ā/hī/k'e/lai* "(lake) was there."

[75] *-me*, postposition.

[76] *q!wAt-*, as in note 73. *da-*, adverbial prefix. *θ-*, second modal prefix. *-t-*, third modal prefix. *-gAc*, verb stem. Verb form ("it lies thrown on top") used as noun.

[77] *nā-*, adverbial prefix. *θ-*, second modal element. *-L!ō*, verb stem. Verb form ("whereon there is writing") used as noun.

[78] *q!wAt-*, as in note 73. *da-*, adverbial prefix. *s-*, second modal prefix. *-L-*, third modal prefix; doubtless original *-l-* changed to *-ł-*, *-L-*, because of preceding *s-*, which in turn is prevented by it from changing to *θ-*. *-nā*, verb stem. Definite past tense.

[79] Analysis uncertain, presumably demonstrative in force.

[80] *mAł-* "therewith" consists of pronominal stem *m-* followed by postposition *-ł-*. *t'e-*, adverbial prefix. *tc!-*, deictic prefix indicating indefiniteness of object. *-t-*, consonant borrowed from following *-ts!*, to complete syllable begun by *tc!-*. *ts!Al-*, apparently passive in force. *-lec*, verb stem. Verb form used as noun: "smoking materials."

txAs/xé/la[81] dṓ/at/t!ī.[82] q!wÁt/tc!At/djā xā́ s/ts!An/na/Ác
He was rich bachelor. "Table quickly he'll bring to me,"

djÁn/la[83] łí/t!ī/ni. dṓ/LAn[84] XWACL/ī[85] djÁn/la dū́/at/t!ī/nì.
said dog-owner. "Not much I believe it," said bachelor.

né/tc!ūc/lec.[86] cṓ[u]/djī.[87] an/γí/aL[88] djÁn/la łí[i]/t!ī/ni tc!ō/γít-
"I'll bet you." "All right!" "Come here!" said dog-owner, he pointed

/siL/la[89] łī q!wÁt/tc!at/dja łát/dAn[90] nAn/náθ/yā/la[91]
with his finger. Dog table once he went around.

xat ye/γát/ne/la[92] mā́[a]/dAn.[93] łá djÁn/la dṓ/at/t!ī/ni
Then he bit it at edge. "Don't!" said bachelor,

t'wī/dé dō/wa/nā́/yan/nAł.[94] dō/wí/la[95] djÁn/la q!wÁt/tc!At/dja
"everything he will upset." "Of course," he said, "table

---

[81] *txAs/xe*, adjective stem "rich;" perhaps related to *wAs/xe* "good." *-la*, verb suffix of probably inferential value.

[82] *dō*, negative. *at* = *at!* "wife." *-t!ī*, noun suffix denoting "one who has." "One who has no wife," i. e., "bachelor."

[83] *djAn*, as in note 64. *-la*, verb suffix.

[84] *dō*, negative. *LAn*, adverb "much."

[85] *xw-*, adverbial prefix. *-c-*, first person singular subjective pronominal element. *-L-*, third modal prefix; from *-l-*, because of preceding *-c-* (cf. note 98). *-ī*, verb stem. Indefinite present, negative adverb preceding.

[86] *ne-*, second person singular objective pronominal element. *tc!ū-*, adverbial prefix; very likely really compound of deictic element *tc!-* (indicating lack of specified object, namely wager) and modal *ō-*, *ū-* denoting future imperative. *-c-*, as in note 85. *-lec*, verb stem. Indefinite present, because of future or slight hortatory meaning: "let me bet with you!" Cf. Chipewyan *tūs/be* "let me swim."

[87] With *cō[u]-*, cf. Hupa *-hw̱ōn̄* "good;" Kato *-cōn̄* "to be good."

[88] *an-*, adverbial prefix. *γ-*, first modal prefix. *-ī-*, second person subjective pronominal element. *-aL*, verb stem. Indefinite tense, used as imperative.

[89] *tc!ō-*, adverbial prefix; perhaps compound of deictic element *tc!-* (object pointed out is not specified) and first modal *ō-* of unknown significance. *γ-*, second modal prefix. *-i-*, connecting element between second and third modal elements, characteristic of third person of definite tenses with *γ-*. *-t-*, third modal prefix. *-siL*, verb stem. *-la*, verb suffix. Definite past; marks point in narrative.

[90] Numeral adverb of *ła* "one." *-dAn*, postposition.

[91] *nAn-* and *na-*, adverbial prefixes. *-θ-*, second modal prefix. *-yā*, verb stem. *-la*, verb suffix. Definite past; refers to definite point of time in narrative.

[92] *ye-*, adverbial prefix. *γa-*, second adverbial prefix. *-t-*, third modal prefix. *-ne*, verb stem. *-la*, verb suffix. According to this analysis, this verb is indefinite in tense, which is difficult to understand. More plausibly, *γat-* may be considered as misheard for *γAt-;* *γ-* second modal prefix. In that case, it is definite past.

[93] *mā[a]-*, noun stem "edge." *-dAn*, postposition.

[94] *dō/wa*, proclitic adverb indicating futurity, probably not with absolute certainty. *nā-*, adverbial prefix. *-yan*, verb stem. *-nAł*, verb suffix. Indefinite in tense, because future in meaning.

[95] Adverb containing inferential *-la*.

dō/wá/An/nā/yan/nAł[96]	t'wī/dé	dō/wa/ł/t'át/nAł[97]	θAk/gwé
he will upset,	everything	will go to pieces,	in fragments

s/ts!An/na/Ác.	ha/xwil/ī/ha[98]	ÁL/tcā/γī[99]	γÁn/na/Ác[100]
he will bring to me.	Do you expect	big thing	he will bring here

ła/mé/q!e/ca.[101]	wAs/xe	łī.	nā/nī/An[102]	nā/nī/An	djÁn/la
all in one time?	Good	dog."	"Stop him,	stop him!"	said

dṓ/at/t!ī/ni.	dō/dā́/q!e[103]	nā/nÁc/An[104]	djÁn/la	łī/t!ī/ni
bachelor.	"Unable	I stop him,"	said	dog-owner,

t'wī	γÁn/na/Ac/t'e[105]	xwAn/né/θiL/ya[106]	djÁn/la	dṓ/at/t!ī/ni.
"all	he will bring here."	"You win,"	said	bachelor

---

[96] As in note 94, except that another adverbial prefix, *An-*, is present.

[97] *dō/wa* and *-nAł*, as in note 94. *ł-*, third modal prefix. *-t'at*, verb stem.

[98] *ha*, interrogative adverb. *xw-*, adverbial prefix. *-i-*, second person singular subjective pronominal element. *-l-*, third modal prefix. *-ī*, verb stem. *-ha*, interrogative suffix. Indefinite present in tense.

[99] *A-*, of unknown significance. *L-*, prefix common to several adjectives. *-tcā/γī*, adjective stem "big."

[100] *γAn-* and *na-*, adverbial prefixes. *-Ac*, verb stem. Indefinite tense, because pointing to future time.

[101] *ła*, numeral stem "one." *-me/q!e*, compound postposition. *-ca*, found also with *ła* alone: *łā^a/ca* "one."

[102] *nā-*, adverbial prefix. *n-*, first modal prefix. *-ī-*, second person singular subjective pronominal element. *-An*, verb stem. Imperative mode.

[103] Adverb containing negative *dō-*. Perhaps *-q!e* is postposition (cf. *-me/q!e*).

[104] *nā-*, *n-*, and *-An*, as in note 102. *-c-*, first person singular subjective pronominal element. Indefinite in tense, because of preceding negative adverb.

[105] As in note 100. *-t'e*, future suffix; here used because idea of futurity is more explicit.

[106] *xwAn-*, adverbial prefix. *ne-*, first modal prefix. *θ-*, second modal prefix. *-i-*, second person singular subjective pronominal element. *-L-*, third modal prefix. *-ya*, verb stem. Definite present in tense.

APPENDIX.

A few Galice Creek words were obtained from Mrs. Punzie, a few Applegate Creek words from Rogue River Jack. These two Athabascan dialects are probably practically identical. *ś* indicates something acoustically midway between *s* and *c*; *r* (tongue-tip trilled) and *l* occur as reflexes of Athabascan *n*; nasalization (indicated by ‘) seems to occur. *k*‘ and *k‘w* are found as contrasted with Chasta Costa *x* and *xw*.

Galice Creek.

ya’/k‘ȧs “seeds (sp.?);” said to be called *bȧ́nax* or *bą̇yu* in Chinook Jargon

tc!a/ba/ȧ́/k‘wa’s “brush used for medicinal purposes (sp.?)”

ʟ!ō‘/dȧ́i “tar-weed” (cf. Chasta Costa *ʟ!ō‘/dé*; Hupa *Lō/daitc*)

yéɫ/γat/ts!ai/yè “sunflower” (cf. Chasta Costa *tc!ᴀɫ/γat/ts!ė*)

gų̇s “camass” (cf. Chasta Costa *gōθ*; Hupa *kos* “bulbs”)

dȧ́l/si “pine” (cf. Chasta Costa *dᴀ́l/si*; Kato *dûl/tcīk*)

lȧ́ /ʟ!i “pine-nut” (cf. Chasta Costa *nȧ́/ʟ!e*)

dé/reś “manzanita” (cf. Chasta Costa *dᴀ/nᴀ́c*; Hupa *din/nūw̱*; Kato *tûn/nûc*)

má’/tś!i “cat-tail” (cf. Chasta Costa *mᴀt/tc!í*)

śáś/da’ “oak” (cf. Chasta Costa *cᴀ́c/dā‘*)

ɫ/dá/ge “acorn” (perhaps misunderstood; cf. Kato *ʟ/taɢ* “black oaks”)

Applegate Creek.

k‘ą́’/tc‘u “goose” (cf. Chasta Costa *xā’/tc‘ú*; Kato *ka*‘)

dᴀ́c/tc‘ù “grouse” (cf. Chasta Costa *dᴀc/tc‘ú*; Kato *dᴀ́c/-tcō*)

dᴀc/l'ê'/tc'u "bob-white, quail"
k!ai'/díc/tca/wè "ruffed grouse, pheasant"
k'án/ta/tc'u "pigeon" (cf. Kato *kwī/yīnt*)
dō/s'Án/ts!a/ya "screech-owl"
sī/tc!e/les "kingfisher"
tc!ȧ/ke/di "red-headed woodpecker"
tcā'/wác/tc(!)e "sandhill crane" (cf. Chasta Costa *sā'/wᴀs/-ts!é*)